"Donna Erickson's elegant and gripping account of her family's experiences ranching on the edge of Missoula . . . has provided a new layer of understanding to the challenges now facing Missoula and countless other western towns and cities. . . . There is nothing easy about the lives of the families Erickson writes about, but it's the irrepressible sense of possibility running through her account of those lives that will help us work our way toward solutions to the challenges now facing our communities."
—Daniel Kemmis, former Speaker of the Montana House of Representatives and former mayor of Missoula and author of *This Sovereign Land: A New Vision for Governing the West*

"Part loving memorial of Donna Erickson's girlhood on Montana's Skyline Ranch, part warning of damages to the land through the forces of development, *Rooted at the Edge* concludes with a feather of hope for western Montana's landscape. Beautifully detailed and evocative."
—Mary Clearman Blew, author of *Think of Horses*

"Rich, multilayered, meticulously researched, and lovingly portrayed, *Rooted at the Edge* is essential reading for mending fences and opening hearts. With her deep roots in the Skyline Ranch and a career in open-space planning, Donna Erickson lifts the blinders that stereotype ranchers and environmentalists. Ultimately, she offers the promise of a new way forward for conservation, like the return of the mountain bluebird—her favorite bird."
—Marina Richie, author of *Halcyon Journey: In Search of the Belted Kingfisher*, winner of the 2024 John Burroughs Medal

"In *Rooted at the Edge*, Donna Erickson beautifully portrays the rich history of three generations of her family's life on the Skyline Ranch, one of three ranches perched in the North Hills overlooking Missoula, Montana. In clear, crisp prose, Erickson explores the intertwining of family, land, and community among these twenty-first-century ranchers. Whether she is writing about riding fence, haying, moving cattle, showing 4-H calves, or working in the family café at the stockyard, Erickson tells an important story of how a family's grit and ingenuity assure survival on the ranch overlooking a burgeoning town. A wonderful addition to Montana literature!"
—Caroline Patterson, author of *The Stone Sister*, winner of a 2022 High Plains Book Award

"Like the Lone Pine of Skyline Ranch, standing sentinel over the author's childhood home of Missoula, Montana, *Rooted at the Edge* draws us together to consider what truly matters as our communities face dramatic changes. The author's pen is on the pulse of life in this mountain valley as it adjusts to changes in technology, demography, and climate. Donna Erickson weaves a soulful web through the decades, then leads us to the edge for a glimpse into the future. So vivid and well-written, even the history of the Missoula stockyards is an engaging read."

—Sally Thompson, author of *Black Robes Enter Coyote's World*

"*Rooted at the Edge* is the story of a woman of the American West who learned to read landscapes on the back of a horse. In a clear, authentic voice, Donna Erickson herds words with the same acumen and determination she developed moving sheep and cattle in her youth, drawing on her experience of her Montana home to tell a universal tale about attachment to place. She inspires us to think about the future of our surroundings with empathy and common sense, and to see how land creates belonging."

—Frederick Steiner, dean of the Stuart Weitzman School of Design, University of Pennsylvania and author of *The Living Landscape: An Ecological Approach to Landscape Planning*

"If you have lived in Montana, you won't be surprised: this ranch child's memoir is smart, succinct, and honest. It is also a fine addition to Montana literature. In style and content, this is a model of personal history. A memoir depends not on what was, on what has changed, or on nostalgia but on style: how sensitive and intelligent is the speaker? We need a well-spoken guide through this forest of the 'was' that no longer is. A voice we can trust, as well as events worth remembering. In every page, this is a voice I trust and respect."

—William Bevis, author of *Ten Tough Trips: Montana Writers and the West*

ROOTED AT THE EDGE

Ranching Where the Old West and New West Collide

DONNA L. ERICKSON

UNIVERSITY OF NEBRASKA PRESS

Lincoln

© 2025 by Donna L. Erickson

CREDIT: Liz Newman, "Of Ruin and Renewal"; David Thomas, "Waterworks Hill," Foothills Publishing.

All rights reserved

The University of Nebraska Press is part of a land-grant institution with campuses and programs on the past, present, and future homelands of the Pawnee, Ponca, Otoe-Missouria, Omaha, Dakota, Lakota, Kaw, Cheyenne, and Arapaho Peoples, as well as those of the relocated Ho-Chunk, Sac and Fox, and Iowa Peoples.

♾

LIBRARY OF CONGRESS CONTROL NUMBER: 2024038736

Designed and set in Arno Pro by Katrina Noble.

Decorative drawings throughout created by the author. Maps throughout created by Hannah Schafer.

Honoring the legacy of my grandparents,
Mildred and Lawrence Kramen,
and celebrating the futures of my grandchildren,
Felix, Jocyna, Sofia, and Sulatda.

Contents

List of Illustrations   *ix*

Acknowledgments   *xi*

PROLOGUE   1

PART 1. THREE RANCHES ON THE EDGE   9

   1. Geology Rocks   11

   2. The Lone Pine   29

   3. Hold Tight to Deeded Land   35

   4. You Can't Eat the Scenery   52

   5. Land Rich, Cash Poor   67

PART 2. STORIES FROM THE EDGE   81

   6. I Pledge My Head to Clearer Thinking   83

   7. Raised by the Land   90

   8. All Livestock Sold as Is   101

   9. Water Runs Downhill   113

   10. Boxcar Blues   122

   11. A Ranch's Rusty Jumble   130

PART 3. FORCES OF CHANGE AT THE EDGE 141

12. Force Times Distance 143

13. Fire Roars Uphill 153

14. Shoot, Shovel, and Shut Up 163

15. The View from Here 172

16. Death and Taxes 183

PART 4. RENEWAL AT THE EDGE 193

17. Gravity Wins 195

18. Bluebird Days 207

EPILOGUE 227

Illustrations

PHOTOGRAPHS

1. Panorama from the top of the Big Pasture toward Missoula Valley 4
2. Aerial of the Missoula Valley 14
3. 1940s elk harvest 40
4. Interior of Murphy's Corner 47
5. Mildred Kramen in front of the log cabin at Skyline Ranch 50
6. Bill Randolph 54
7. Winter scene at the homestead 64
8. Archie Carlson 71
9. Missoula County Fair in the 1920s 88
10. Author with her horse Blue 94
11. Spurlocks at the Trail Café 105
12. Harriet Spurlock and calf, 1970s 128
13. Ranch items at Montana Antique Mall 135
14. Rye and Reed on their pony Cappy 137
15. Stoneboat 145
16. Rock hanging from fence wire 146
17. 1940s haying with horsedrawn equipment 147
18. Ranch house in the 1940s before the yard was created 155
19. Scenic view of North Hills from downtown Missoula 174
20. Barn demolition and intact harness shed 198
21. 1940s putting hay into barn's loft 203

ILLUSTRATIONS

1. Urban-wilderness transect   185

MAPS

1. Crown of the continent ecosystem   12
2. North Hills and its surroundings   17
3. Skyline Ranch, Hellgate Ranch, and Moon-Randolph Homestead   21
4. Skyline Ranch   48
5. The Homestead   58
6. Hellgate Ranch   76
7. Conserved land bordering Skyline Ranch   180
8. Skyline Ranch split into 20-acre and 40-acre parcels   185
9. 2020 hike destinations   209

Acknowledgments

I wrote these stories over fifteen years, bolstered by a four-woman writing group formed to nurture the nonfiction books that pulled at our hearts. This work would not exist without my partners at the "Rockin R"—Beth Judy, Marina Richie, and Sally Thompson. They repeatedly asked for more of "me" in the writing and saw, earlier than I, the important connections between my personal and professional stories. They helped me move from a style of academic writing toward prose that is, hopefully, more engaging.

Wendy Ninteman shepherded this book, with a big heart and a keen eye, from conception to birth. Nearly twenty years ago, we discussed the themes of this work; and she was there at the end to help it take its final form. Thank you!

My poet husband, John Koenig, was my "first reader," chapter by chapter. His insightful sense of language, nuance, and tone helped bring life and emotion to my work. I appreciate your patience with this long and arduous project.

My family members love Skyline Ranch and the North Hills. Some of them read early versions of my work, provided important details, corrected my faulty memories, and encouraged my storytelling. I am indebted to Betty Miller, Richard Miller, Rye Hall, Reed Hall, and Harriet Spurlock, though any holes or mistakes in these stories are mine alone.

Other readers, advisers, and supporters gave me critical feedback, corrected my ungainly prose, and reminded me of important details. Enormous thanks to Don Erickson, Liz Gupton, Robert Grese, Craig Hall, Daniel Kemmis, Edie Kieffer, Nancy Seiler, Lynn Tennefoss, and Jim Walker.

Cynthia Morris was instrumental in helping me finalize the manuscript and launch it into the world. Then it came to life with the brilliant assistance of my editor, Clark Whitehorn, and others at University of Nebraska Press. I appreciate Hannah Shafer's cartography skills and Stephanie Marshall Ward's careful copyediting.

The University of Montana supported my work by funding illustrations, through its Matthew Hansen award. The Missoula Public Library's non-fiction writing award encouraged me, specifically endorsing the chapter "I Pledge My Head to Clearer Thinking."

Finally, I am grateful for teachers who have shaped my thinking about landscapes and helped me communicate through writing—Fritz Steiner, Julie McQuary, Hubert Van Lier, and the late John Forssen.

ROOTED AT THE EDGE

Prologue

You never know what events are going to transpire to get you home.
—Og Mandino

My son Rye and I visit Skyline Ranch's highest point by exactly the same route but with different vehicles. Rye, twenty-nine, fights forest fires throughout the West from his base in Oregon and trains each spring for the grueling summer fire season. As he grinds his mountain bike slowly uphill, he's wearing his weight vest with its many pockets, each holding a two-pound weight. He's probably carrying an extra forty pounds today. It's April 2004, spring break from my teaching, and I've coordinated my trip from Michigan to overlap with Rye's. We've rarely gotten the chance to visit the ranch together in recent years. I drive my mom's beat-up Forest Service–green 4x4 a comfortable distance behind Rye, crawling along the two-track road until we get to a steep hill. Then I pass him and holler, "Lookin' good! See you at The Top," out the window. He's huffing and sweating, pulling in a low gear. I know I'll be alone for a while as he labors uphill, but spending time up there always calms and soothes my spirit, in a bittersweet way.

We are heading "over The Top," shorthand in our family for traversing, whether by foot, bike, horseback, or 4x4 pickup, a big circle from the ranch buildings up over the east–west ridge line of the North Hills—above Grant Creek on one side and the Rattlesnake drainage on the other. The ridge, with its scattered ponderosa pines, is the top of what my family calls the Big Pasture, a one-square-mile fold of hills visible from downtown Missoula, Montana. If it were fall, we might see the North Hills herd of elk, up to a couple hundred head, grazing on dried bunchgrass.

This ridge is truly an edge—the place where the dark forest falls northward for a half mile or so then rises toward the wilderness. At the high point of the ridge, I get out and walk a short distance to the edge of the steep hillside. I scan the city and the ring of hills and mountains circling it, a view I've enjoyed by horseback hundreds of times. A slight haze blankets Missoula today. It's not uncommon for air inversions to trap air in the valley; in a couple of months smoke from wildfires in the surrounding mountains will linger there.

Rye and his bike look tiny as they enter the Big Pasture at the Four Corners far below. This geography is coded in place names for us: Four Corners, the Basin, Big Pasture, the Saddle, the Hundred and Sixty, the Lone Pine, Lookout Hill, the Meadow, the Lower Spring.

In the middle distance, I recognize most of Skyline Ranch's main landmarks, even though the ranch buildings are hidden behind a hill. The buildings of the other two North Hills ranches are also invisible due to the lay of the land, but their rolling pastureland forms the middle-ground. The Carlson and Randolph places lie south and west of Skyline Ranch, respectively. Far less lovely, Missoula's landfill is also part of the North Hills scene and, from my vantage point, looks like a large white blot on the landscape, with festering stitches carved in the hillsides angling out from sealed scar tissue.

The long view south is out past the North Hills, over Missoula to the Bitterroot Mountains. We are at nearly the same elevation as Mount Jumbo, which creates the eastern edge of the Rattlesnake Valley. This iconic Missoula landform looks like a sleeping elephant, its rump at the Clark Fork River and its trunk pointing north to the Rattlesnake Mountains.

I moved away from Missoula on New Year's Day, 1980, and for the past twenty-four years I've come back to the ranch for a few days in summer or at the Christmas holidays. I always feel as connected to the land as to the family. During our first eight years away, my two young sons, their dad, and I lived close enough that I could visit more often. The boys rode horses and provided "gopher" services for weeks at a time in the summer, which cemented their attachment to both the ranch and their grandparents.

Later, we returned less frequently from our homes in the Netherlands, Wisconsin, and then Michigan. Ironically, the longer I am away, the stronger my attachment to the ranch feels. Gradually, I sensed the ranch changing as my parents aged. Eventually, they got out of the cattle business and stopped raising horses, relying completely on off-ranch income. Now other peoples' cattle graze at the ranch in the summer, and one elderly horse roams the hills alone. No one puts up hay, and the fields grow to weeds. Since my dad died last fall, the end of one chapter for the ranch is even more certain. It is increasingly painful to see the place lose its vibrancy. Although this has always been marginal ranch land—best for grazing livestock, not raising crops—a lot of tasty fruits and vegetables have come off the place over the past century. The ranch seems to be going dormant, waiting for new life.

As the ranch has changed, so have its surroundings. As I look out in spring 2004, development is closing in on two sides. I see new houses going up at the ranch's edges, although the Carlson and Randolph places have stayed undeveloped. People want to live in and near these hills, particularly in the neighboring Grant Creek and Rattlesnake Creek valleys. This view from The Top now includes ranchettes that are neither part of Missoula nor truly part of the North Hills. In my time away from Montana, I've seen sprawling development at the edges of many towns, and I worry about the future of the ranch if Missoula sprawls northward. Still, landscape change is incremental. The view today is not startlingly different from last year.

Rye joins me after a half hour, drenched but happy. The big payoff awaits: most of the ride back to the house is downhill, and he'll get there long before I do. But for a while we just sit quietly soaking in the view. We perch on a fifteen-foot ponderosa limb downed by a recent lightning strike. I marvel at the tall bluebunch wheatgrass up here, a big change from the days I worked

PHOTO 1. The view looking south from The Top of the Big Pasture. The North Hills are in the foreground, City of Missoula in mid-ground, and the Bitterroot Mountains in background. Photo by Richard Miller.

cows in these hills. In recent years only a few cattle have grazed here, so the grass grows thigh high, even though thistles and other weeds are starting to take hold. As Rye rides off again, I hear the grasses hiss through his spokes. I stay at The Top a bit longer, watching him swoosh downhill, through the Basin and the Four Corners and across the Hundred and Sixty. He'll cover the two miles to the house in mere minutes.

On the ridge, the air is lighter, sweetened by the aroma of the pines and the sound of a soft breeze in the trees. A red-tailed hawk launches from one of the pines above me and circles away to the south. Up on this higher ridge, the yellow-orange sunflowers are just starting to bloom—or that's what my family always calls the native arrow-leaf balsamroot. Nearly three feet tall in places, the showy blooms will cover the hillsides in splashes of gold at these highest elevations of Skyline Ranch. Buttercups and shooting stars are in full bloom. I sit in the grass and hear buzzing bees. I lean back to examine the undersides of sunflower buds.

The view is much as it was when the Scandinavian farmers first settled these North Hills. At least the scene in the middle-ground is the same; however, on the flat valley floor, Missoula's houses and commercial areas spread much farther to the south and west, even climbing the lower slopes on the South Hills opposite my viewpoint. But the grassy hills, treed ridge lines, and graceful swales of the North Hills are just as they were when my grandpa put his cattle out in the spring on good bunchgrass.

Sitting at The Top, I view the ranch through both personal and professional lenses. Since 1989 I've worked as a professor of landscape architecture at the University of Michigan. Landscape architecture combines art and design with an understanding of the ecological and social values of land and water. I am attracted to that combination, which connects me directly back to the ranch. I teach graduate students about land-use planning and open-space conservation in rural places. I conduct research that asks where to expand urban areas while protecting vulnerable agricultural land, examining the forces that shape rural places, particularly at the margins of towns and cities.

When I bring my profession to bear on Skyline Ranch, I look out on the Big Pasture and see habitat, open space, ecological corridors, and viewsheds. I understand its combination of vulnerability and great promise. And I am not alone. The City of Missoula and several land conservation organizations have tried to prevent this land from being developed. When the Rocky Mountain Elk Foundation's national office was at the edge of downtown Missoula, its employees literally kept a close eye on the ranch. Employees set a telescope in the front window, trained on the Big Pasture and the elk using it as winter range. The foundation was interested in that land staying open for grazing elk.

My academic expertise about the ranch overlaps my personal feelings about the place, tied up in family legacy, childhood experience, and a hands-on working knowledge of getting by in the North Hills. All of that is complicated by living nearly two thousand miles away, as well as by family

PROLOGUE / 5

dynamics. I dread the onslaught of new housing in these hills; it's like waiting for a silent, menacing force to arrive.

Driving the pickup down in Rye's wake, I pilot a course through high grasses that camouflage the route. I'm feeling my way on the not-quite-road, barely a two-track, hitting a rock here and a badger hole there. I know every subtle landform as I drive past the water trough, along the lupined hillside, and below the high-voltage power lines. I cannot count the times I've navigated those ruts, or ridden as a child in the truck bed, jumping out to open gates for the adults. But knowing this land stems even more from a childhood and early adulthood wandering these hills on horseback.

Closer to the house, I drive across flatter ground—a hayfield planted by my grandfather that, for decades, produced good alfalfa hay. Bucking hay bales into a truck bigger than the one I'm driving now comes to mind as I think of the hot summer days of my child and teen years. Back home in Michigan, while driving down some country road later this summer, I'll have the window rolled down and smell newly mown alfalfa. That sweet, earthy aroma will instantly take me back to this field. The visceral connections—to the place, to the people, and to work itself—always return me to childhood. For many years, the smell evoked guilt: I wasn't at home to help put up the hay.

WHEN THAT SUMMER rendezvous with Rye ended in 2004, I flew back to Michigan and he drove back to Oregon. As my plane tilted into the sky at the end of the runway, I looked out the window and could see the North Hills, a lovely muffler between Missoula and the wilderness. Looking at it from the air, seeing its whole shape and the definition of its periphery, I understood where it fits inside me, what space it fills, how it forms a core piece of who I am, where I have been, and where I will go. It is achingly hard to leave, and I know I want to influence what happens to this piece of ground.

I moved back to Missoula in 2005, just a year after my outing with Rye. Leaving Ann Arbor was a big risk; people rarely leave tenured professorships at major research universities to start fresh outside academia. The ranch pulled me home but was only one of several motivations for the move. I did not come back to live a ranching life. But returning was a creative urge—a desire to integrate the personal with the professional, to combine old and new loves in ways that felt meaningful.

When I left Ann Arbor, I packed up the voluminous piles of paper that a professor accumulates—boxes of administrative files, course materials, scholarly articles, and what seemed like a truckload of books— but I chose not to sort through all of it or to carefully eliminate what was extraneous. I brought it all with me.

NOW IT IS 2018—thirteen years since I left Ann Arbor to come home. I can see the Big Pasture regularly when walking downtown from my house in the city. I'm flushing out the academic files to make more room and to finally tear threads that bind me with that former life. What I save from this flood of paperwork is as good a measure as any of my persistent interests and passions. Single reprints of articles I wrote are filed away; they represent years of funded research. And I can't seem to part with the material from my graduate education in the Netherlands, where I studied the careful planning and design of rural lands reclaimed from the North Sea.

As I make the piles, I realize that I've come full circle. I keep everything that pertains to planning rural lands. I'm not done with it. As I sit on my stool, sneezing over the dusty paperwork, I know that this topic is what motivated me professionally in the first place. It circles back to the North Hills, to that ridge line over Missoula's northern skyline and to my intimate knowledge and love of that piece of ground. The ranch and my background on it have shaped my professional interests, but now that profession is shaping how I feel about and understand the ranch. Attachment to a place is complicated and contradictory. Like loving a person, love of land is, on the one hand, calming; it steadies the soul. But because the land is a living, breathing place, part of that love is also risk and struggle.

This is the story of Missoula's North Hills, three families who settled there, and a western community that has, over time, been both supportive and challenging. I seek to dig deeper than family legacy. Lifestyles change.

People come and go. The land stays, immovable, silently waiting. The history of these edge ranches typifies hundreds of western places caught in the schism between the old and new West, and the generations of families drifting between them. North Hills stories apply to other towns that were once nourished by farmlands at their edges but now consider paving them.

PART 1

THREE RANCHES
ON THE EDGE

1

GEOLOGY ROCKS

A place belongs forever to whoever claims it hardest, remembers it most obsessively, wrenches it from itself, shapes it, renders it, loves it so radically that he remakes it in his image.
—Joan Didion, *The White Album*, 1979

During the years I lived outside Montana, I could easily explain where I was from by mentioning an image from a popular movie. In the opening credits of *A River Runs Through It*, the camera pans across the Missoula valley from the south for a couple of seconds, revealing the 1950s-era town, the hills north of Missoula, and the Rattlesnake Mountains beyond. The movie viewer can glimpse the timbered ridge line of Skyline Ranch in the North Hills, my family's land, bridging town and mountains.

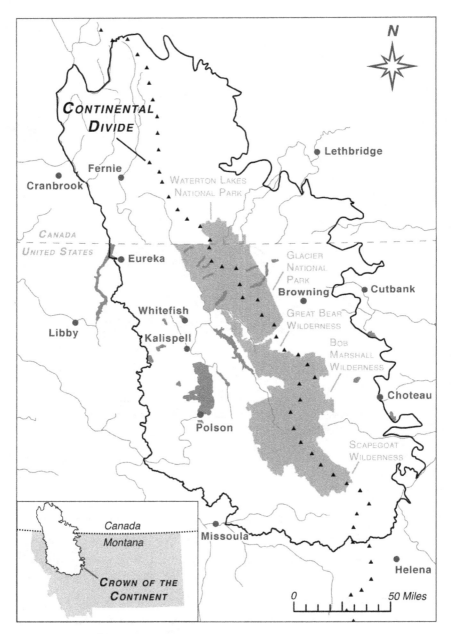

MAP 1. Crown of the continent ecosystem

What is not clear from the cinematic view is that those hills are the very foot of a vast landscape—the Northern Continental Divide Ecosystem—that is one of the last, largest undeveloped regions of the lower forty-eight states. It encompasses almost 10,000 square miles of northwestern Montana, including Glacier National Park, four wilderness areas, parts of two Indian reservations, and five national forests.

Missoula sits in the hub of five valleys and the Native trade routes that fan out from them. The rivers create a valley pattern—Bitterroot, Blackfoot, Upper Clark Fork, Lower Clark Fork, and Mission. The town nestles between mountain ranges west of the Continental Divide. Missoula, in the Salish translation meaning "Place with Bull Trout," specifically references the confluence of Rattlesnake Creek and the Clark Fork of the Columbia River, where European settlers started a trading post in 1858. Several protective mountain arms wrap around the Missoula valley. The town grew up along the banks of the Clark Fork River, spreading into the fertile valleys where the Blackfoot and Bitterroot Rivers converge with the Clark Fork. A 1999 *American Heritage* magazine named Missoula "The Great American Place." In that article, Fred Haefele wrote: "nourished by powerful rivers and an equally powerful sense of its past, a town of cowhands and poets and bikers and professors distilling the whole history of the American West—its hope and rapacity, its calamities and triumphs." Missoula has been making "best of" lists ever since for any number of qualities and quirks. With over 75,000 residents, it is considered the cultural hub of Montana. It is growing rapidly.

On three sides, a skirt of dry, rounded hillsides frames the flat urban expanse that was the bottom of Glacial Lake Missoula 12,000 years ago. Lake Missoula filled and drained dozens of times between 15,000 and 13,000 years ago. Water marks from those ancient shorelines show up as subtle horizontal lines across hillsides surrounding town. Mount Sentinel, at over 5100 feet high, forms the eastern edge of the valley and rises about two thousand feet above it. These steep, mostly treeless hills provide the fabric for the University of Montana's "M" embroidered on Mount Sentinel and Loyola High School's "L" on Mount Jumbo, each stone landmark on its own expanse of steep, grassy terrain. The painted letters provide orientation; a quick glance up from the valley helps me

PHOTO 2. Aerial view of Missoula, Montana, in November 2019. The view is north toward the Rattlesnake Wilderness. The city is embraced by the North Hills (to the left) and by Mount Jumbo and Mount Sentinel on the north and east sides of town. A distinct edge separates the city from these scenic hillsides. Photo by Julia Malich.

determine cardinal directions. On the other hand, the hills can deceive and confuse me with their shape-shifting in response to weather patterns or the angle of view. The "M" sits high on Mount Sentinel's flanks when you look east from the university, but look toward the "M" from farther south and you clearly see that it is situated only a third of the way up the mountain, if that. The shifting perspective sometimes confuses our sense of direction. South of town, scars rake the side of Lolo Peak, so it appears gouged by giant bear claws. Trees were cleared for ski runs, but the ski resort never materialized. From some angles, that scene seems to be in the southeast.

Missoula's hills appear brown for much of the year, and Missoulians become giddy in those few May and June weeks when the hillsides stay soft lime green, with new growth poking through last fall's buff, dry grass. The steeper land beckons us up from the valley floor year round, but especially in those early summer months.

The North Hills rise abruptly from the town's northern edge. It is a Sunday in September 2009, and I've decided to join an adult-ed geology class. I trek up to get a different perspective on an area I know well from childhood. Five women and one man—all middle-aged—trail Bruce Baty up Waterworks Hill, the hill closest to town, across the ridge of Randolph Hill and toward Skyline Ranch. Bruce retired from teaching high school earth science a few years ago and enjoys sharing his geology knowledge in adult education field trips. Although it is officially fall, the temperature is nearly 90 degrees, and we carry water and sunscreen as we climb the dry, exposed ridge. We are dressed in shorts, sleeveless shirts, and hiking shoes; Bruce wears a "Geology Rocks" T-shirt.

While Bruce talks, we look out and then down at our feet and then out again, studying both the plants and rocks in our shadows and the landforms at the horizon. We squint in all directions, but we also scan back and forth in time, considering formations millions of years ago, coming forward to what we see now, and going back again. Bruce points out Ch-paa-qn, (pronounced "cha-pock-kwin"), which translates to Salish-Sleeping Woman, far to the west—a pyramid-shaped peak bordering the Flathead Indian Reservation. Below us, ancient, meandering waters scoured out the Missoula valley and

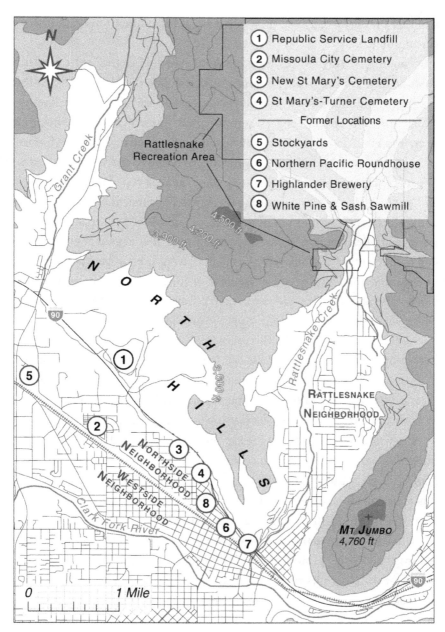

MAP 2. North Hills and its surroundings

whittled the many canyons, draws, and small valleys that flow into it from surrounding hills.

Standing on Waterworks, a wedge of the North Hills that pokes into the city, we view the geographic boundaries that define the North Hills on the east, north and south. We are too far east to see the narrow Grant Creek valley, which forms the western edge, where suburban homeowners are converting former ranch land on rich bottomlands to upscale housing. Although most of Missoula's new housing development is trending to the wide-open west, housing is climbing north as well—up onto the hillsides of the Grant Creek and Rattlesnake valleys—squeezing the North Hills ranchers. We face north and I like Bruce's description of the hills as "rumpled." He explains that the geological phenomenon of "rotational slumping" has caused the rumpling, and with it a mosaic of different soils that, in turn, affect vegetation patterns. The slumping is a downward movement of rock and soil that keeps whole blocks of material intact. We see irregular, wavy patterns across the ground where slight shifts in slope, soils, and moisture alternate across the hills.

Farther north, the North Hills merge into steeper, more forested country, becoming the Rattlesnake National Recreation Area, designated by Congress in the early 1980s, which then segues into the Rattlesnake Wilderness. Colors morph from the brown hills into forest green in the recreation area to the green-black and snow white of distant higher peaks in the wilderness.

The wilderness area, the highest protection the federal government can impart, is part of the wild country stretching north all the way to Glacier National Park, harboring grizzly bear, wolves, and elk. Ice Age glaciers carved this alpine landscape, moored by Stuart Peak, our main landmark looking northward. The North Hills form a critical transition zone from the growing Missoula urban area to the pristine wilderness beyond it. Many American cities, small and large, protect greenways connecting riparian areas, neighborhoods, or the city to its rural hinterland. A few cities, such as Jackson Hole, Salt Lake City, and Tucson, lie close to designated wilderness. But Missoula may be the only city in the United States where a hiker can walk on public land from its urban core into a federally designated wilderness area a mere four miles away. Or take a city bus! The #5 Mountain Line route drops a hiker at a trail leading into the recreation area.

The public enjoys this footpath on the ridge of Randolph Hill, beating it into a line that's visible on Google Earth. The trail is one of the most popular in Missoula's open-space system. We can see where hikers and dogs have swelled the 1.5-foot-wide trail to over 4 feet in places, trampling on the sensitive plants that grow here. Exposed ridges with shallow soils support a cushion plant community—plants that grow low on the ground, forming cushion-like mats, including Missoula phlox, which has white to light blue flowers, and *Douglasia*, blooming in pink and purple. We can see these blushes of color from town in April. Missoula phlox is designated as a "species of concern" and found in few other places on earth. Like the bitterroot, our state flower, these cushion plants are well adapted to wind, drought, hot sun, and shallow soils—all plentiful in the North Hills. The wind-swept ridge lines are water-stressed from almost constant wind, which reduces the amount and effectiveness of any available water. But over the past decade, this habitat is being loved to death, threatened by overuse along the trail up Waterworks and Randolph Hills.

To the east, the narrow Rattlesnake Valley embraces a desirable Missoula neighborhood, connected to Missoula by fourteen-mile-long Rattlesnake Creek, which starts high in the wilderness and flows south into the Clark Fork. Steep Mount Jumbo, only a few hundred feet lower than Mount Sentinel, encloses the narrow valley on its eastern side. The valley allows recreational access to the public land beyond but has long provided other, more basic, resources to the city. When the Northern Pacific pushed its rail line through Missoula in the 1880s, a local lumberman stripped timber from unclaimed land in the upper Rattlesnake to create railroad ties. Those ties anchored rail lines stretching ten to fifteen miles in both directions from Missoula. As I stand on Waterworks Hill overlooking the mouth of the valley, I imagine teams of work horses pulling wagons loaded with logs, heading to a mill. After cutting the square eight-foot ties from the logs, railroad workers floated them down the Clark Fork River to their destinations.

I stand on a flat bench of land near the squat, domed tank that stores a million gallons of water originating in the Rattlesnake Wilderness, giving Waterworks its name. The Rattlesnake water supply is less important in recent years but was the primary source during much of Missoula's history. In the 1880s two city leaders organized the first water plant up here. They built two wooden reservoirs, supplied with water from lakes high in what is now the wilderness. Wooden flumes carried the water for miles to this point for storage and distribution to the early town. Missoula now relies on the Missoula Valley Aquifer, far below us, as its water source.

The trail's first uphill half mile traverses private land, on which landowners generously allow public access. We reach the apex of Randolph Hill farther along the ridge, a fairly short hike, but we are an hour or more into our excursion because Bruce stops often for short lessons. He describes the unique geologic strata in these hills, including coal, clay, and volcanic ash. Fossilized leaves of sequoia, cottonwood, alder, willow, and aspen lie at the bottom of the ash, fifteen to twenty feet below our feet. Paleontologists have found about five hundred known specimens of plant fossils in the North Hills. It is fascinating to get this insight about what lies beneath a surface landscape I know so well. I am aware of the black and white—coal in some places and ashy pumice soils in others. But I am ignorant about the volcanic origins and the evidence of a marshy prehistoric landscape below it. From the high point on the ridge line, we walk gently downhill, northwest a bit farther, toward the three places that define the North Hills for me—about three thousand acres of ranchland. We can see two sets of ranch buildings. The third, the Randolph place, is below us, but its buildings are too close to the base of the hill to be visible. The ranch land defines this region for my mother too; she is the one who first used the term North Hills in a conversation with a county commissioner. The name stuck.

Bruce points north toward the route of a now-invisible east–west trail that Native Americans created long before European settlement. In the pre-Columbian era, the Missoula valley served as a natural hub for the many trails used by Salish, Pend Oreille, Kootenai, and Nez Perce people. The people thrived here from time immemorial. In the spring, Native peoples gathered in the Missoula valley to dig the prized root of the bitterroot for a First Foods

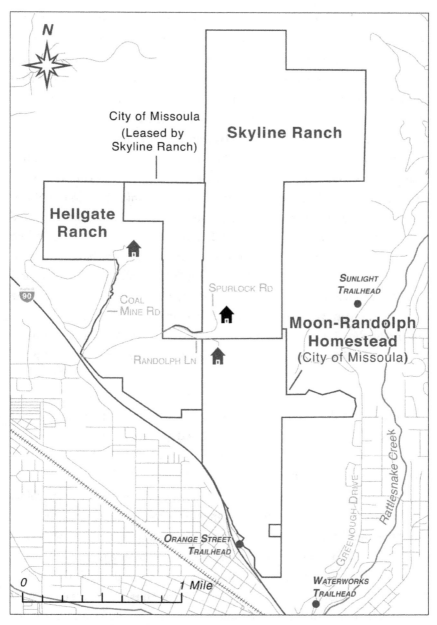

MAP 3. Skyline Ranch, Hellgate Ranch, and Moon-Randolph Homestead

Feast. They made camps in protected draws, which brought them into the North Hills. With the introduction of horses in the 1700s, the trails became broader and more prominent, just as our heavily used trail is widening with increased use now. Members of these tribes traveled twice a year to buffalo hunting grounds east of the Continental Divide, and the road through the Missoula valley became known as "The Road to the Buffalo." It cut across all three ranches that occupy the North Hills in modern times.

Now, limited vehicular access makes the North Hills ranches a small community. The ranches fall within Missoula County, near the city-county boundary. Coal Mine Road connects the three places and links them to the North Side neighborhood. The road starts near an industrial zone, ducks through a freeway underpass, and then forks to Missoula's landfill before dead-ending at the Carlsons' Hellgate Ranch. Another spur heads from the freeway east and uphill to Skyline Ranch and the Randolph Homestead, forks again, and dead ends at each. We follow the trail north to its end, looking down on the forked gravel road. When we reach the fence line separating the city-owned land and Skyline Ranch we go no farther. The city owns the Randolph place and installed a sign with an important distinction in the North Hills: "End of Public Access: Private Property Beyond This Point."

As we make our way back along the ridge and down Randolph Hill, we face Missoula to the south. Today the city splays out in a panorama, but it often hides below a layer of fog or haze created by weather inversions. Before the 1980s, smog from a pulp mill west of town cast a hazy blanket over the valley, and the city was often invisible from the North Hills.

Back on Waterworks Hill, we raise our voices above a jarring freeway whine. Interstate 90, one of only two interstate freeways traversing Montana, needs no identifying number for locals. "The freeway" forms a seam between Missoula's North Side neighborhood and the North Hills. It follows a physical divide as well. Bruce points out an invisible line where the Ninemile Fault runs across Mount Jumbo's saddle and west across the North Hills. Faults create straight lines, which are unusual in the natural world; this one defines the northern edge of the Missoula valley, a line made visible by the freeway. Bruce assures us that no evidence exists of the fault moving within the last few million years.

22 / THREE RANCHES ON THE EDGE

The freeway, completed through Missoula in 1966, added to the list of what planners call LULUS—Locally Undesirable Land Uses—in the North Side. The North Side has long been bordered by industrial development— sawmills and other wood-product manufacturers, rail yards, and stockyards. The freeway split the North Hills from the neighborhood in both symbolic and tangible ways. It cut off North Siders' easy access to the hills that had served as a large backyard for decades. Freeway construction also demolished fifty-eight homes, which included small farmsteads and orchards. The tall Garden City Brewery, built in 1895, brewed popular Highland beer and nosed up against the base of Waterworks Hill directly below where we stand. Freeway construction bulldozed it. Warehouses lining the railroad yards stored and sold wholesale produce grown across the extended Missoula valley. Those facilities closed after trucking replaced rail transportation.

Dave Thomas, a local poet, eloquently captured the experience of being at the spot where I'm standing.

WATERWORKS HILL

Bluebird perches
        fence post
darts
away
a flash of sky
    as I walk
    this well
    traveled road
late morning sun
cutting sharp
shadows
few trees
    bunch grass
    in short clumps
wildflowers about

Missoula spreads
   Below
Full of early summer
   Leaf
and Saturday bustle
window glitter
   brick shine
I-90
A concrete ribbon
     of roar
       and reflection
Orange Street
   and its bridge
the Rail Link/BNSF
     switchyard
and mainline tracks
a barebacked
   stroller
with small dogs
   crunches
gravel
   the micro
     wave
relay tower
   a gentle
   breeze
birdsong
pierces
the vast rumble
   of traffic
the hidden
   thunder
of a jet plane

Lolo Peak
    White
against
hazy blue
    sudden
    bang!
of a shunted
    freight car
    the simple
majesty
of the land
    spouting
summer
in all its varied
      green
my inky
scratches
    mingle
with insect buzz
    a quiet
    breath
this fence post
fallen and rotting
into the still damp
      earth
invites me to sit
    feels
    home
for a moment
before I trudge
      back
below
walking stiff

kneed
downhill
a harrier hawk
rises
tiny grasshoppers
jump
at my every
step.

—Dave Thomas, *Waterworks Hill*, 2010

After its completion in 1883, the railroad separated the North Side from downtown, and access from one side to the other has been problematic ever since. As in many western towns, the Northern Pacific Railroad became Missoula's hub in the early twentieth century, with a bustling commercial area just south of the tracks and three working-class districts radiating from it—the West Side, between the railroad and the Clark Fork River, and two neighborhoods, the lower Rattlesnake and North Side, north of the tracks. For eight years I attended Lowell Grade School on the West Side, walking over the tracks on what we called "the viaduct." The lower Rattlesnake neighborhood, where Rattlesnake Creek opens into the Missoula valley, attracted higher-paid railroad workers by the 1890s. The lower Rattlesnake neighborhood, about twenty square blocks north of the freeway and the railroad, is now designated as a historic district.

What is now the Northside Railroad Historic District was the first expansion from Missoula's original townsite. The North Side neighborhood was largely built for newcomers, housed in "railroad worker houses." Greeks, Italians, and other immigrants helped maintain the rail yard. Anchored by local grade schools, the modest neighborhood housed blue-collar workers. The historic register nomination states that "these ethnic bonds, coupled with occupational cohesiveness of railroad employment, lent the Northside a sense of neighborly identity that was perhaps the strongest in Missoula."

Even before the freeway existed, Missoulians considered the North Side the wrong side of the tracks, making it estranged from the rest of the city. Now the freeway wedges it in even further. The Missoula landfill, dug into the North Hills just north of the freeway in 1969, doesn't help that image. Garbage trucks heave through the North Side continually. "Landfill" is the more polite term, but we called it "the dump," our ranch's neighbor from my high school years on.

The seven of us look down on the empty triangle of land where the railroad's round house, switching yard, and machine shops once employed hundreds of workers, a few blocks east of where the viaduct once stood. A larger, abandoned industrial site lies at the western edge of the neighborhood. The White Pine and Sash Company, a sawmill and window and door manufacturer, anchored the North Side neighborhood from 1917 to 1996, hiring hundreds of North Side and West Side workers. I recall passing by the bustling mill every day as shifts changed and workers came and left with their metal lunch boxes. The city is slowly reclaiming the contaminated forty-acre site for soccer fields, playgrounds, and commercial uses. Near it, industrialization has intensified, with huge fuel storage tanks and trucking yards.

You cannot drive to the North Hills without passing at least one of three cemeteries—the Missoula Cemetery, St. Mary's Catholic cemetery, and its annex a mile away. The first two older sites are lovely landscapes with mature trees and narrow paved lanes—benign compared with other North Side LULUs. And the North Side is experiencing a renaissance. Industrial chic is trendy: from our vantage point on Waterworks Hill, we can see an arts center in a restored historic building, a produce warehouse converted to a brewpub, small new homes on narrow lots, and a greenway trail hugging the tracks. The North Side is reinventing itself into a hip, but affordable, place to live, even though it still houses workers of modest means and young families. Any new North Side–North Hills connection will be crafted partly by new generations of North Side residents. And the connection centers partly on the trail on which I stand. Hundreds of people hike up Waterworks Hill to get a different perspective of the valley and to enjoy the open, high ground.

GEOLOGY ROCKS / 27

The three ranches form my North Hills mental map, a neighborhood of pioneering families who settled here in the late nineteenth and early twentieth centuries. The land is central to the identity of five generations of North Hills families, who have faced constant battles with scarce water, abundant rocks, fire danger, drifted roads, invasive weeds, trespassing urban neighbors, steep slopes, and marauding dogs. "Geology created some of those challenges," Bruce explains to his band of middle-aged learners. But others come with proximity to a growing urban area. Although the North Hills are separated from town—higher, dryer, more exposed—they have always been linked to forces starting in town. For earlier generations, that force was providing food and employment for townsfolk. Along the way, the North Hills became a place to dump garbage. Now it is in demand for its scenery, wildlife habitat, and hiking trails. Those assets depend on special geological forces that help explain the relationship of these hills to the valley below. The dichotomy between practical and amenity values sets up tensions affecting how the North Hills will be valued in the future.

The urban-rural fringe is valuable, resource-rich, and vulnerable. Across the west, we see increasing homogenization of the landscape. Rural lifestyles are compromised by suburbanization, economic hardship, and family dynamics. A way of life and a way of work are vanishing. Ranchland may be simultaneously cherished by a family for the life it has made there and coveted by urban neighbors for open space. Community residents may love a place for its scenery and wildlife habitat, while others are happy to convert it to a Walmart parking lot. Complex ecological values can be destroyed in one afternoon by a bulldozer. Statistics about development and the loss of ranches at the urban fringe do not fully convey all that is lost. When we add the threats posed by climate change and shifting populations, the edge becomes even more compromised.

2

THE LONE PINE

The ache for home lives in all of us, the safe place where we can go as we are and not be questioned.
—Maya Angelou, *All God's Children Need Traveling Shoes*, 1986

On the warm September morning of my dad's funeral, in 2003, we held a graveside service at the Missoula Cemetery, within sight of the upper reaches of Skyline Ranch. My grandmother honored these views with that name. Her ranch, the Kramen place, became Skyline Ranch eighty years ago. It is fitting that we can see these hardy symbols of the ranch from my dad's resting spot, since he worked the ranch for half his life. Scattered pines are draped across the Big Pasture's shoulders in the North Hills, appearing almost black from this distance. They grow on the dry southern slope, thriving in full sun. The trees sketch a graceful dark line where they seek a little more moisture in the ranch's two big draws.

Bud was my stepfather, but I called him Dad from the age of three, when he married my mom. After his memorial service, a dozen of us went back to the ranch and up to the Lone Pine. Some relatives, like my cousin Judy and me, hadn't seen each other for over twenty years. We drove the quarter mile to the tree in my parents' rig, kids bouncing in the bed of the pickup like the old days. We parked on a knoll, walked to the tree, and strolled around it, talking, mourning, and soaking up the late summer sun. The more agile among us, like my firefighter son, Rye, climbed the tree and looked down on us and out across the Rattlesnake Valley.

The tree is a ponderosa pine. It's my family's "heart pine." In woodworking, the phrase is used to indicate old-growth wood that is denser, more tightly grained, and stronger than fast-growing timber. Old-growth features in the wood begin to appear when the tree is about middle age—a hundred years or more in the case of ponderosas. I don't know the age of the Lone Pine; its heart is measured in other ways—as a symbol of the ranch and our family over time.

A named living thing gathers its own lore. Five generations have cherished this tree and its location—at the same time sheltered and open—as a sacred place. Fitting, as ponderosa is the Latin word for "heavy, weighty, or significant," referring to the tree's impressive size and stature. The Lone Pine grows on the top of a small knoll with its back to a larger hill. I realize that trees don't really face one way or another, like a Christmas tree in the corner of the living room with its "good" side turned outward. But to me, the Lone Pine faces east, only feet from the eastern fence line of the ranch. We share this landmark, knowing that it has meaning for Rattlesnake Valley residents as well. They can clearly see this sentinel on the ridge above them; the tree is one symbol of the North Hills.

If elk are the charismatic megafauna of the North Hills, the ponderosa pine, or "P Pine" as the locals call it, is the charismatic megaflora, although grass is the dominant native vegetation. Ponderosas have many other nicknames, such as bull pine, used to describe young, fast-growing stands. On the highest ridge of the Big Pasture, stately ponderosas grow in park-like groves, easily recognizable by their shape—straight, tall trunks topped by an open, irregularly shaped crown. The bark of the older tree becomes orange-brown, organized in large, flaky plates like jigsaw puzzle pieces. The mosaic of plates stands out against the black furrows between them where the bark splits. Native Americans ate the ponderosa's seeds and created dug-out canoes from its logs. They used its pitch to waterproof baskets, repair canoe leaks, make ointments for back pain, and treat boils. They peeled the outer bark back to harvest and eat the sweet inner bark.

We love the ponderosa pines in two different ways—as a community and as one individual. The timber in the Big Pasture is special, but more as a community than as individuals like the Lone Pine. We take visitors to enjoy the view from The Top over the Missoula valley, a scene framed by big old ponderosas. It is where we enjoy hillsides of arrow-leaf balsamroot in the spring, watch the two hundred–head North Hills elk herd in the fall, or scare up ruffed grouse in the winter. Birds love ponderosa stands. and it's common to see mountain bluebirds, raptors, and great horned owls.

The Lone Pine, not a particularly stunning specimen of Montana's state tree, is the place for family ritual. It is not tall and dignified: a mature ponderosa pine averages 100 to 150 feet tall, with majestic limbs angling out and up. Stately trees in their prime, ponderosas turn into beautiful gnarly snags when they die. Unlike those up on the ridge of the Big Pasture, the Lone Pine is more squat and wide, about fifty feet tall and with a trunk three feet in diameter. Like all ponderosas, it flaunts spectacular buckskin-red bark and graceful needles, packaged in bundles of three. Its lower branches are easy to reach, whereas many ponderosas its age have lost their lower branches and don't provide quite as much shelter or climbing potential. My dad and I used to collect pine cones here, for making Christmas wreaths or to burn as kindling. The ground is sprinkled with so many it's hard to walk without crunching the heart-shaped cones that radiate a warm nutty color.

My grandparents named the tree as they ate picnic lunches under its boughs in the 1940s and 1950s. My Norwegian grandfather was a proponent of the short digestive nap after lunch. I imagine him dozing on a plaid blanket spread on a bed of tawny needles, the vanilla fragrance from the sun-warmed bark wafting down. The pine scent is known for having a clarifying, uplifting, and invigorating effect. My aunt, now ninety-four, tells me that the Lone Pine sheltered her and her first boyfriend as they shared an initial kiss back in the mid-1940s.

Through the 1960s and 1970s, I rode horseback to the tree hundreds of times, a private place for contemplation and peace. On that September day of Dad's funeral, Judy and I recalled the tree as an important landmark in our youth. I often rode bareback to her house in a subdivision just over the hill in the Rattlesnake Valley. She'd swing on and we'd ride double back to the Lone Pine, tie the horse to a branch, and climb the tree. My mother, as a child, had traced the same route, riding even farther across Rattlesnake Creek to see friends who lived on a small dairy on the flanks of Mount Jumbo.

Those casual horseback trips from the ranch into the Rattlesnake are impossible now. Large houses pepper the land in what seems a random pattern, a common sight at the edges between Missoula and once-productive ranch land. However, in the twenty-first century, I value newer traditions for honoring the Lone Pine. I walk, with my niece and nephew riding double on an old horse, to the tree at Thanksgiving to gather cones.

Cattle once grazed this landscape, keeping the little ponderosa sprouts from taking hold. On our side of the fence, cattle, sheep, and horses have rarely grazed here over the last couple of decades; on the other side, forty-acre rural estates with large homes have replaced livestock. Although the tree was solitary when my grandparents named it, it now has small offspring close by. Since grazing stopped, baby ponderosas have sprung up, widely spaced on the slope. Some are probably thirty years old and ten feet tall. The Lone Pine stands aloof from its seedlings, higher and more pronounced, still proud on the skyline. Right against the fence line, creating a buffer between the ranch and the houses, the city of Missoula maintains an open space corridor with a public trail.

The physical landscape of the North Hills, despite the suburban development to the east and west, is relatively unchanged from decades ago, when three families made modest livings here in ranching, mining, and timber—the three-legged stool of Montana's economy before tourism added a solid fourth leg. Two of those families continue to live in the North Hills. A third has passed on and Missoulians own and enjoy its land. These three places are known to some Missoulians, although the three sets of homestead buildings are out of view from the valley floor. They are a half mile from town as the crow flies, and yet separated distinctly by steep hills. The tucked-away location is symbolic, since these families have always valued privacy from their nearby urban neighbors.

Life in the North Hills has always been a matter of just making do. Farmers patched up old machinery to get a few more seasons out of it, holding things together with baling wire and amateur welding. My dad married into Skyline Ranch and made it his own over a forty-year period. He was tall, dark-haired, of medium build, and wiry as he got older. An introvert by nature, he did like to laugh and tease. With little formal education, he was widely known as a jack-of-all-trades, capable with carpentry, wiring, plumbing and horse training, among a dozen other skills. My parents supplemented their ranching income with other pursuits but always considered themselves ranchers. These hills on the edge are not quite ranches, and not quite town either. The proximity to town changes everything. Ranch land here at the edge is, at the same time, vulnerable and valuable—vulnerable if we want the landscape to stay intact and undeveloped. And, of course, valuable for development. I remind myself constantly to enjoy the ranch for what it offers now.

In the winter of 2014, a weather fluke created a special scene at the Lone Pine. A harsh, wet winter had created a glassy skating rink in the swale just west of the tree. It formed when deep snow melted quickly in a typical January thaw. Water a foot deep froze solid since it could not melt into the ground or run off. Another skiff of snow covered it—perfect for skating after a bit of shoveling. Rye just happened to find the 30-foot-by-60-foot ice sheet when hiking. None of us had ever seen such a perfect rink develop in the ranch's many small valleys.

Rye, his daughters, my niece, my mom, and I spent a memorable winter afternoon around a bonfire as the girls and Rye skated in the shadow of the Lone Pine. My then seventy-eight-year-old mother used a hiking stick to help ascend the slope up to the tree, just forty feet from the fire. She stood, a dark silhouette beneath the tree in the waning light, with her back to me and looked out over the Rattlesnake Valley. After a few minutes, the cold drew her back down to the fire to watch her great-grandchildren skimming the ice.

My mother and I savor these unique, sweet moments that the ranch offers. We both know that everything has changed here, that a portion of the ranch died with my dad, as it did when her parents died. Human mortality is a marker of uncertainty about the land. How will it be used? How will it coexist with Missoula? Will it stay in our family? Perhaps my grandchildren and their descendants will know and love the ranch and the Lone Pine as the generations before them have. Maybe the Lone Pine—the century-old sentinel at the edge—will continue to survive, grow, and reproduce against all odds, a landmark for people in the valley and a family's heart pine. Remarkable headway must be made in collaborating with the town next door.

3

HOLD TIGHT TO DEEDED LAND

> The land belongs to the future... How many of the names on the county clerk's plat will be there in fifty years? I might as well try to will the sunset over there to my brother's children. We come and go, but the land is always here. And the people who love it and understand it are the people who own it—for a little while.
> —Willa Cather, *O Pioneers!*, 1913

My family's eighty years is a millisecond in the natural history of Skyline Ranch. However, owning it has shaped the family's course and impacted Missoula's welfare. Four generations have called it home—literally home at different times in each person's life, but a place we all come back to. A fifth generation did not start out there as mine did but still loves the place.

Our family raised food to make a living, yet the ranch was always much more than a business.

The ranch has lived through a recurring progression of phases, parallel to its owners. In the ranch's infancy after homesteading, settlers slowly built up the infrastructure for ranching. Then for about seventy years the ranch was lively, productive, and expansive. Its produce and meats fed people in town. Middle age brought focus, a narrowing of activity. Elderly ranchers closed in even more, no longer able to go through the hard work of calving, haying, and mending fences. As living waters that swell and recede through yearly seasons, the ranch's vitality and energy ebbed and flowed over a century in tandem with family histories. A critical question in the early twenty-first century: what is the next phase of the ranch's evolution and how will that relate to the city?

At the ranch, home is not a house, but the land itself. For my mother, and her parents before her, a basic tenet of life is holding deeded land. Pride of ownership is fundamental. In today's world, land is often just another asset, a commodity to buy and sell. In my family, it's a one-way proposition—buy it and hold on tightly. As I watch the arc of my family's story, as well as my own inclinations, I am amazed how this trait persists and shapes our view of the world. I see this best through my grandparents.

My love for the ranch and for my grandparents went hand in hand. To a large extent I was raised among adults. I had a half brother eleven years younger, but no other children nearby. Those formative years at the ranch were both a luxury and a limitation, teaching self-reliance and many hands-on skills while also preventing much of a social life. I spent a lot of time with my grandparents at the ranch before school age and then lived there full time with my parents from the age of ten. My grandmother, Mildred Kramen, was a skilled homemaker. Her artistic sensibilities wore off on me. I was in 4-H from the ages of nine to nineteen, an activity that reinforced my recordkeeping habits but also encouraged domestic and artistic interests. At twelve, I signed on for a Home Grounds Beautification project, foreshadowing my interest in landscape architecture much later. I planted trees, grew sweet peas to climb the stile, painted the yard fence, pruned an apricot tree, and tended perennials my grandmother had planted—irises, columbine, poppies. Away from the house, I roamed the North Hills alone, usually on horseback, for most of my youth. I knew every small gully, hard-to-open gate, and watering hole. I felt the sharp poke of wild hawthorns in the big draw, heard newborn lambs bleating in the night pasture, and tasted fresh-picked raspberries from the large garden.

I come from a line of recordkeepers and diary makers. My grandparents recorded their lives in a series of meticulous journals from the 1930s to early 1950s. The pile of dusty old ledger books with dirty gray-green covers rested on shelves at the ranch house for decades. I recently found and read those journals to deepen my understanding of my grandparents, long dead, and to supplement childhood memories and stories from my mother and aunts. Through the early 1940s the Kramens recorded every penny spent on gas and truck repairs. Lists of names and addresses show an egg delivery schedule for the North Side and West Side neighborhoods, with notes by the orders of twelve dozen or so: "having a party" or "wedding." The records show purchases of louse powder, socks, and turpentine, each costing only a few cents. On one page, between tallies of truck expenses for 1944, in his fluid European hand, my grandfather Lawrence recorded the big purchases of his life and tally of his work.

Feb. 26,1941. Final payment on house $19.44 at cost of $1305.85 as bought May 7, 1931.

April 8, 1935. Date employed at Bonner for A.C.M. Company. Quit November 27, 1940.

November 22, 1938. Purchased 1936 International Truck. Weight, no load 5470 lbs. (Mileage 1900) Cost $506.00, Used. Capacity 1 ½ Ton. Box 7'×12'.

Behind the cryptic notes are years of toil, tears, laughter, and worry.

Grandma almost never raised her voice. Activity and work defined her life, but she also had an eye out for fun, a soft-hearted kindness, and an interest in music and art. She wore her long, thick red hair braided, out of her way as she worked as a helpmate to her husband and mother to three daughters. As a child I remember brushing her hair to a soft luster while standing behind the hard-backed kitchen chair where she sat.

Born in 1909 in Tekoa, Washington, one of twelve children, she grew up in Montana from the age of three and lived here until her death at sixty-six. Her husband, Lawrence, recalled spotting her frequently in the mid-1920s on the #50 streetcar, which looped around Missoula, past the University, and east to the mill at Bonner. That old #50 is now on display in its own barn at Fort Missoula. Mildred was still a high school girl living with her family when Lawrence rode #50 back and forth to Missoula. He worked as a lumberjack in the Blackfoot's Anaconda Copper Mining Company (ACM) Camp #5, but on his days off he stayed at widow Hilda Johnson's boarding house in Milltown. The short, stocky Norwegian had Americanized his name from Lars Kvammen to Lawrence Kramen.

Lars's parents immigrated to America at the start of the Klondike gold rush in 1896. They met on the ship and married. Lars was born in Iowa the same year. His father went on to the Yukon, where he hauled men and supplies over White Pass, a less risky business than mining gold. The small family returned to Norway in 1898, when Lars was only two. He was an American citizen when, at sixteen, he returned to America for good in 1912. Since he was the oldest son, leaving meant giving up his inheritance on the family farm in Norway. He worked on movie sets in California and in the fields of the Imperial Valley, before coming to Montana.

Lawrence and Mildred met in 1929, a few years after he first glimpsed her. She attended a dance with her brother, and Lawrence quickly fell in love with the beautiful red-haired girl whom he had admired on the streetcar. They married in 1930 and just months later purchased a modest two-bedroom house from Lawrence's sister on Missoula's West Side, a working-class neighborhood wedged between the Northern Pacific tracks and the Clark Fork River. In the depression years of the 1930s, Mildred gave birth to their three daughters at that Howell Street house, tiny by today's standards. Betty was born in 1931, Martha in 1934, and Harriet, my mother, in 1936. Even though Lawrence was born an American, by heritage, culture, and language he was Norwegian. He was intent on becoming a true American and tried to put the "old country" behind him. He insisted on speaking English and, for the most part, refused to teach his three daughters Norwegian. My Aunt Betty remembers that she would ask him to translate words into Norwegian and then she'd learn them. But when a word came up that he could not translate he said, "Oh, to heck with this. We're in America now! We speak English." That was the end of Norwegian lessons.

Lawrence worked in the ACM lumber mill at Bonner with many other Scandinavian and French immigrants. My mother's birth certificate lists his occupation as a "cant hook man." A cant hook is a traditional logging tool with a wooden handle connected to a movable metal hook, used for lifting, turning, and prying logs. Logs often filled the Blackfoot river bank-to-bank as they swept downstream to the mill. The intrepid cant hook men jumped and danced between the bucking tangle of logs to keep them moving and prevent log jams. The work was dangerous and demanded incredible strength and agility. When a cant hook man fell into the river, he rarely came out alive among the roiling logs.

As the country came out of the depression, opportunity was slim but the Kramens did not consider themselves poor. They owned a home and a car and always had food on the table, including game and fish that my grandfather gleaned from western Montana's mountains and streams. The Howell Street house sat on a quarter acre of land bordering the railroad tracks—a tiny farm really—on which they raised a big garden and kept a milk cow, pigs, sheep, and chickens. A shack on the alley served as a small barn. They also owned horses, pastured in Pattee Canyon on Missoula's south side. The family kept the horses for pleasure riding but, even more importantly, for hunting. Over many years, Lawrence brought dozens of elk and deer out of Montana's mountainous terrain on the backs of horses.

Like his father before him, Lawrence hauled goods for people to make ends meet. Throughout the depression he cut, hauled, and sold firewood, first

PHOTO 3. Elk harvested in fall 1950 from what is now the Rattlesnake Wilderness, hanging at Skyline Ranch. The hunters are Lawrence Kramen and his nephew Warner Lundberg. Photo by Mildred Kramen. Author's family collection.

using a Model A and then a 1936 International truck. When he worked nights at the mill, he was hauling both firewood and garbage during the day. Lawrence started hauling garbage in Missoula neighborhoods the day his first child was born and quit the day she turned eighteen. He used to say that after paying the doctor for her birth he had twenty-five cents in his pocket. This was the early years of the Great Depression. There were five men hauling garbage in Missoula in the 1930s. Before the U.S. entered World War II, a hauler named Matty Service left Missoula for the shipyards on the coast. Lawrence immediately went door-to-door to Service's customers, offering to haul their garbage. His ambition and enterprise yielded all of those accounts. From about 1935 to 1940 he worked nights at the Bonner Mill, toiled three days a week on the garbage route, and hauled firewood on the side. He would go to the mill after dinner, work until 2:00 or 3:00 a.m., sleep a few hours, then go out on the garbage route. Finally, once they had paid off the mortgage on the Howell Street house, he was able to quit the mill job.

In the early years of the business, he shoveled garbage off the truck by hand into the Clark Fork River just west of the Orange Street bridge, a common practice as late as the 1970s. He was proud of his trucks, but even prouder of the hoist he bought in 1941, which allowed him to dump, rather than shovel, garbage from the truck. He could work faster, expand the business, and take on new accounts. Mildred often rode in the cab of the truck with him, collecting payments at back doors in the first week of each month and emptying cans into the truck when he couldn't find a hired man during the war. Her diary includes many entries about "working at our business." Their daughters still know Missoula streets from riding along as their father emptied cans in alleys throughout the growing town.

Lawrence was fiercely ambitious, hardworking, and set in his ways. While he was bigoted about people unlike himself, he didn't want anyone to call him a foreigner since he was born in the U.S. His dream was to own ranch land in western Montana, a place he found so similar to Stordal Fjord on Norway's mountainous western coast, where he grew up. The Kramens scrimped and saved through the depression and World War II. Long before recycling was the norm, and certainly before "upcycling" was in vogue, he rescued brown Highlander beer bottles from the trash. His daughters washed them, and Mildred returned them to the brewery at the base of Waterworks Hill for a few coins. Lawrence roofed the garage with old tin signs nailed with the lettering side down. Rather than buy worms for fishing, Lawrence raised them in a washtub by the back door. I have the small wire basket, with a handle, into which my grandmother put soap bar fragments. When swished in water, soap pieces created suds for washing linens. My family's thrift persisted long after the depression.

At last, the Kramens had enough money to buy our family's ranch on March 31, 1945, just before the end of the war. They paid Jonas Suneson $5000 for 160 acres, and Lawrence's ledger book shows that the final payment was made less than a year later, on January 5, 1946. How proud they must have been to hold that deed! They now owned a "quarter section," the acreage of the original homestead parcels—a half mile on each side. As more land was added to the ranch in later decades, the family always called that original 160 acres the "Home Place."

I grew up with the vague mystique of the Sunesons. I almost thought of them as ancestors. Jonas Suneson farmed in the North Hills for nearly fifty years; he was eighty years old when he sold his place. Lawrence called him The Swede or Old Man Suneson; there was surely some of the legendary Swedish-Norwegian rivalry between them. Lawrence was forty-nine and Mildred thirty-six. My grandparents allowed Jonas to continue living in the house for a few months as they made a gradual transition from Howell Street to the ranch. Aunt Betty remembers "the big old man sitting on a chair near the stove and the kitchen table. He wasn't very talkative. The rest of the house was closed off. This was spring of 1945." Eventually, Mildred grew uncomfortable with that arrangement, and Jonas spent the last months of his life in Missoula. I'll never know if leaving the ranch broke his heart.

I wanted to know more about Jonas, so I contacted his grandson Al, retired and living in Polson, Montana. He recalled his grandfather as a storyteller and "pretty good farmer." Born in 1865, he immigrated from Sweden, with an older brother, at the age of eleven or twelve. He purchased his North Hills land in 1898 from Charles Smith, the first non–native born occupant, who had claimed a homestead in 1891. The 1862 Homestead Act mandated that homesteaders "prove up" on their quarter section claims by living on the property, making improvements, and transforming often marginal land into productive agricultural ground. Smith acquired his deed in 1896, the year of my grandfather's birth, but stayed only two more years before selling.

Jonas's wife, Selma, gave birth to their son Coit in 1903 after losing two infants. After twelve years living in a two-room, shed-roofed cabin that faced south, Jonas built a solid home of native lumber in about 1910. The two-story, four-bedroom frame house looks out to the western Missoula valley from a wide front porch. This was no make-do handmade affair: Suneson hired union carpenters from Missoula to construct it. My mother and I both grew up in that house. Jonas used the original cabin as a chicken coop. Like Jonas had many decades earlier, I cleaned the coop, fed and watered hens, and gathered eggs in the old building where he had started his little family. And like him, I sold eggs on Missoula's North Side.

Jonas was physically strong, a barrel-chested man. He had a reputation for successfully treating injured and sick livestock, particularly horses. According to Al, one time a cow Jonas had sold escaped its new owners and walked back home, a story one usually hears about cats and dogs, not cows. The Sunesons tended an immense truck garden, between the house and the barn, and, like the Randolphs and Carlsons, planted a fruit orchard. They grew large fields of truck farm produce—rhubarb, raspberries, and asparagus—which they sold in Missoula. Missoula's truck farms inspired the "Garden City" nickname that Missoula has long enjoyed. Jonas never owned a tractor but harvested wheat with a team of horses. He minded milk cows and laying hens. He sold milk, fryers, and eggs.

Like me, Jonas's son Coit was lonely on the isolated ranch in his youth and missed playing with other kids. The farming life didn't stick with Coit, at least not directly. After earning an agronomy degree in the 1920s, he worked in California and never again lived in Montana. In 1940 he visited his father's ranch for the last time, with family in tow. Al Suneson tells me "the family of five camped in tents and sleeping bags out by the barn, rather than staying in the big ranch house. At the end of the visit, we couldn't say goodbye to Jonas because, before we woke up, Jonas had picked a crop of raspberries and left in his Model A Ford to sell them in town." His frugal ways were legendary. Coit once said, "When I get out of here, I'm going to get a dog." Jonas was so frugal he wouldn't feed a pet.

After Coit left in the 1920s, and especially after Selma's death in 1932, Jonas's farming enterprises narrowed to his orchard crops and truck garden patches. He continued to sell eggs, but he no longer grew field crops of hay and grain. When the far younger Kramens took over, the ranch entered another period of expansion. As the name Skyline Ranch connotes, the ranch was a scene of beauty, optimism, and hope.

For about five years after buying the ranch, the Kramens continued their garbage-hauling business and used the Howell Street house as a primary residence. They needed the hauling income, but, as self-employed people, they

HOLD TIGHT TO DEEDED LAND / 43

had the flexibility to take an afternoon drive to the Bitterroot Valley to look at a horse for sale, or to do some fencing at the ranch. Life at the ranch was more rustic, as electricity was not available until 1952, the year I was born. The family used kerosene lamps—everyday lamps Monday through Saturday and a more ornate Sunday lamp. The girls were allowed to carry the everyday lamps from room to room but were not to touch the Sunday lamp.

Eventually the Kramens turned their full attention to the ranch, where they started building up a herd of white-faced Hereford cattle and worked at many other farming enterprises—milk cows, chickens, and a truck garden. My mother, Harriet, remembers, "I was so happy to now be a milkmaid rather than the garbage man's daughter." My Aunt Betty sold ranch produce to the Missoula Mercantile. "There was a little red and white grocery store that faced East Front Street. They bought all the asparagus and rhubarb I could bring on my bicycle." My grandparents sold the Howell Street house to Betty in 1951 when she was twenty.

Inside the front cover of one journal, I find a note: "Skyline Ranch House 3560, Pond 3763." Although they are unexplained, I quickly recognize these numbers as elevations. The pond was an important feature on the Home Place, where water was in short supply. Its location was highly unusual: at the top of a ridge east of the house. Water from the pond has been critical for many decades. Coit and Jonas Suneson dug a trench from the pond to irrigate fruit trees and gardens; my mother still uses pond water to irrigate trees. My grandpa fenced it to keep livestock out and kept it cleaned of algae and debris. He used a "tumble bug," a horse-drawn dredge with an iron scoop. As a child, Mom led the horse to help her dad with this chore.

The journal lists birthdays, including those of their neighbors William and Emma Randolph. The Kramens continued to track every income and expense, from the amount of rye seed planted in each field, to the numbers of hay bales fed to the cattle each winter day, to the prices and weights of every yearling calf sold. They penciled in detailed records for each cow. Their names were poems of creativity, whimsy, and pride: Sunfish, Round Butte, Swan River, Moonlight, Pancake, Echo, Windy, Zero, Roughneck, Skyline Lady, Kate Smith, Chicago, and dozens more.

Mildred's diary reveals her pride in the ranch and a passion that probably contributed to their buying the ranch in the first place—horses! She and I bonded at the intersection of horses and art. I have old horse sketches that each of us penciled on long winter evenings. Many of her diary entries repeat the theme of going to the ranch to feed, groom, ride, and train horses. Others record excursions to examine horses for sale, a favorite pastime, and books she read about horses. Horses were on her mind a lot. March 12: "Milk man stopped and talked horse to me. Then I called Mrs. Schotts and talked horses to her."

Her diary from the first half of 1946, when they owned the ranch but were still in the hauling business, sheds light on their busy double lives. The winter months include many references to the difficulty of getting to the ranch through snow and mud on a narrow dirt road winding up from the North Side. They often had to put chains on the truck at the bottom of the hill, winter drudgery that was common before Montana winters became milder and the county plowed more. Skiing at the ranch is also a repeated theme. When I was growing up, the garage rafters cradled the skis that my grandfather used. Years later I inherited the old wooden slats. I learned to ski by sliding my insulated work boots into the simple leather bindings on the plain wooden skis and pointing downhill from the front of the house.

In the spring of 1946, Mildred wrote about planting potatoes, beans, and corn. In April they planted pine trees, Chinese elms, and more fruit trees. The family also began building the facilities they needed for a cattle operation, such as fencing and corrals. By May, they were getting an irrigation system in place. May 24: "We went up to the ranch and started connecting pipes and I helped them till time to get dinner. . . . They got the pipes all laid out and tried them out. Boy we sure have got it now. All the water we need for the garden from now on, and some for the hay field."

Mildred was a self-described introvert. Her diary records meals cooked and eaten at the ranch house but almost always mentions "going home" to Howell Street in 1946. The cooking entries evoke the smells and flavors of her magnificent baking—butter horns, cookies, apple pies, cream puffs, angel food cakes, rhubarb pies, freshly baked bread, crullers, and birthday cakes. I remember sitting on a high stool watching her mix dough and chatting about horses. Although she was a caregiver and provider, she was also self-sufficient. One of her diary entries sums up her delight with the ranch and her ability to enjoy it alone. She took a respite to the ranch on February 12: "He (Lawrence) got cranky so I decided to go up to the ranch for a vacation. It does him and the kids good to get along without me once in a while." Over the next couple of wintry days, she fed and groomed horses, read, carried water to wash a few clothes, and cleaned up the house. February 16: "Got up—started fires and went out to feed horses. It is beautiful up here today. It looked like millions of diamonds on the snow when the sun shone on it." This was an independent attitude for a woman in the 1940s. In addition, her diaries show that she was thinking about painting and other artistic pursuits long before she was able to develop them for herself.

My grandmother's daily life was shaped by whether her husband had a hired man for the day, and the quality of that help. She was back-up labor, accountant, and active business partner. The figures in the big journals show, in her hand, records of payments, taxes, and expenses. Her diary entry for January 21, 1946: "Daddy worked at business—had a no-account man." She records those unsuccessful hires as well as the days he had a reliable hired man, the days she went along because the help quit midday, showed up drunk, or didn't show up at all, and the places they went in search of a helper.

My grandfather hired day labor at Murphy's Corner, at the corner of Spruce and Higgins in downtown Missoula. Today that corner is the Iron Horse Brew Pub, packed on the weekends, with people lined up at the bar and munching nachos and burgers at tables inside and out. Missoulians end their work week with a local brew. The Iron Horse was named for its proximity to the north end of Higgins Avenue, where Missoula's main drag dead ends at the railroad track. Near that junction, a large steam locomotive—iron horse—rests as a reminder of the railroad's influence on this mountain town.

This corner has been raucous for many decades, long before the Iron Horse existed. This is the edge of the former Skid Row, paralleling the tracks. Since at least the 1930s, a bar called Murphy's Corner served beer to earlier generations of strong young men loitering around this corner, some looking for work. Murphy's Corner was a landmark on the seamier side of town,

PHOTO 4. Interior of Murphy's Corner at Higgins Avenue and Spruce Street in downtown Missoula. Photo taken in the 1950s. Archives and Special Collections, Mansfield Library, University of Montana.

although during prohibition it served as a grocery and sandwich shop. A photo taken inside Murphy's Corner in the 1940s shows its tin ceiling and the cluttered dark wooden back bar with a Prince tobacco sign. The big mirror reflects a stuffed mountain lion on another wall. When I was young, a typical kid's prank was to answer the telephone by yelling "Murphy's Corner!" In the early 1940s, when my grandparents sent their oldest daughter downtown on an errand from the West Side, they instructed her to walk on the south side of Spruce Street, not on the side of Murphy's Corner.

Unemployed men, sometimes coming in on the rail, hung around looking to earn a few bucks. Other farmers and ranchers in and near the Missoula valley hired migrant laborers from Mexico to work in the sugar beet fields west of town or the orchards in the Bitterroot. Day labor from

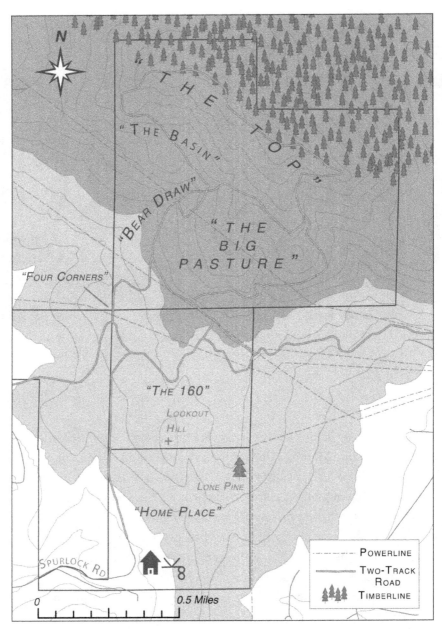

MAP 4. Skyline Ranch

Murphy's Corner was even less organized. It was a cash system, and it relied on a certain understanding between employer and employee. Values were not always compatible, and the men came and went. The ledger books show that a few worked for two or three days, but most stayed just one. Labor flowed as another commodity, like meat, vegetables, and eggs, between Missoula and the North Hills.

In 1951 the Kramens bought nearly a square mile—560 acres—of higher ground, providing the capacity to graze about one hundred cow-calf pairs. This is the land my family has always called the Big Pasture. Another 160-acre quarter section of land separated that land from the Kramens' homeplace. An old family of Missoula nurserymen owned it and harvested topsoil from it— that dirt being another North Hills product for Missoula. This parcel, which we unimaginatively call the Hundred and Sixty, is lovely, treeless land—with undulating steep, dry hillsides and small hidden valleys on the east and a flat grassy bench on the west. My family used the Hundred and Sixty long before they bought it in 1987—another legacy of my grandfather's stubborn ambition. In the 1950s Lawrence built a half mile of barbed-wire fence on the eastern side of the Hundred and Sixty—separating this land from the upper Rattlesnake Valley. He had no formal agreement about grazing his cattle there and did not obtain permission to build the fence He reasoned that since he was allowing access through his land for hauling topsoil, he could graze his cattle on this neighboring land. The owners let my family graze this quarter section for forty years after Lawrence's bold decision.

The Kramens leased the 120 acres to the west of the Hundred and Sixty in the 1950s, calling it—surprise—the Hundred and Twenty. Good grassland, it is now owned by the City of Missoula with a conservation easement protecting it from any future development. The easement lists open space resources, including scenic, historic, and ecological values as motivations for protecting it using public investment. My mother continues to use it with a lifetime lease.

Grandpa died of cancer in 1961, when I was ten years old, passing on a legacy of Scandinavian traits—stubbornness, pragmatism, and pride. My memory of him is vague, but infused with warmth, security, and love. He owned Skyline Ranch for less than twenty years. It is fitting that the city

PHOTO 5. Mildred Kramen standing in front of the log cabin at Skyline Ranch in June 1963. The outside walls of the cabin were adorned with antlers from game harvested by Lawrence. Photo by Betty Kramen Miller. Author's family collection.

dump landed in the North Hills only a few years after Grandpa died, given that garbage helped him buy the ranch. He sold his garbage-hauling business to a family who, years later, created the landfill.

Grandma blossomed after Grandpa died. She took a course to learn oil painting; in one of her letters from the 1970s she was courageous enough to refer to herself as an artist. She became a member of the Montana Institute of Arts, learned to drive, and, in 1964, earned her nursing certification. She lived in a log cabin on the ranch for a couple of years but then moved to a small house in the lower Rattlesnake neighborhood and lived there until her death in 1975, when I was expecting Rye.

My mom and dad, who had been living in Missoula, bought the ranch the year before Grandpa died. We moved into the big ranch house that Suneson built and continued to pasture Hereford cattle. We added sheep and raised registered Appaloosa horses. The 1960s through 1980s became another period of stretching and growing at the ranch. My parents bought the Hundred and Sixty in 1987, forming contiguous ownership of nearly 888 acres at Missoula's doorstep (with the use of another 200 as long as my mom lives). Activity and production at the ranch narrowed again as my parents aged. My mother has lived there most of her life and has owned the land for over sixty years. She has never considered selling one acre of it. She is now in her late eighties, and land ownership still transcends most everything else.

Each generation at Skyline Ranch adds a new layer of innovation and enterprise, limited by the land's inherent resources. A transition has been underway during my lifetime—from an era of ownership and production as a way to get by to an era of stewardship. The ranch is passing into an era where habitat for elk is more important than acreage for cows and horses. The scene that *A River Runs Through It* featured, the North Hills as buffer from city to wilderness, may now be the most important thing. This is not an easy transition at any of the three North Hills ranches.

At the family level, the land generates some of the same responses, experiences, and feelings for each successive generation. I'm thankful that my family has written those down. The name remains primary—Skyline as a field of vision, implying enduring perspective and a hopeful prospect and, at the same time, defining limits.

4

YOU CAN'T EAT THE SCENERY

I have 414 acres which I have put up 80 tons of hay. And plenty of pasture for my 30 head of dairy cattle. I raised 40 early spring pullets... I have sold 50 doz eggs a week since the first of Feb. I raised a surplus of garden and potatoes to sell. I had a big crop of raspberries and cherries to sell. There will be 50 or 60 boxes of apples to sell. I took about 800 lb of honey from 10 hives of bees.
—William Randolph Sr. 1944

A breeze blew in from the west, spinning a whirligig on its post outside Emma and William Randolph's back door, generating power for a single light bulb inside. Across rural America, the whirligig is folk art, with hundreds of variations—a wooden cutout of a man chopping wood, a horse galloping, or a woodpecker tapping a tree. The Randolphs' whirligig was one of many creative devices that kept life humming in the North Hills during the first part of the twentieth century. Like the whirligig, homesteaders there responded to the weather and stayed in nearly constant motion. They relied on makeshift solutions and made do with little. And a few optimistic souls were able to spin with those natural forces rather than against them.

Early homesteaders in the North Hills measured success by what "came off" the land. Remarkably, the Randolphs, our nearest neighbors, coaxed many products from their place over almost ninety years—milk, beef, honey, eggs, coal, berries, apples, potatoes, and more. Looking at the brown hillsides from town, the average Missoulian would never dream of the smorgasbord of food produced in those hills. But the Randolph place is now valued more for what "stays on" the ranch—scenery, habitat, and heritage. This is a critical distinction in addressing the future of places like this nearby town.

Bill, Emma and William's youngest son, was a quiet, withdrawn man, never seeking the slightest attention. He lived his entire eighty-four years, until his death in 1995, on the homestead his parents had settled, getting by on very little. He spent his last forty years living alone after his parents died, tending his goats and keeping to himself. Bill was our closest neighbor. A shrubby draw, running east and west, separates Skyline Ranch from the Randolph place. The houses and barnyards cluster on either side, not even a quarter mile apart. The land slopes up on each side of the draw, so we could see many ranch activities on the Randolph place, and they could see ours. When I was growing up, it seemed there was always a lot of activity on our side—rounding up cattle, riding horses, branding parties, cars and trucks coming and going on the dirt road. It was always much quieter on the Randolph side.

Our kitchen window faced south toward the Randolph place. As an adolescent, I often sat by the black wall phone on a high stool, daydreaming while gazing out that window. I thought the Randolph pasture uphill from the orchard was fenced in the shape of a deer's head, and I somehow took comfort in looking at it. We shared a party phone line with Bill, so on that same stool I learned to quietly lift the receiver and listen for someone talking before dialing. It was usually free, but Bill's conversations had long pauses, so I was never sure if he was actually on the line. Decades later, I still almost

YOU CAN'T EAT THE SCENERY / 53

PHOTO 6. Bill Randolph on Brownie in August 1950. In the background, the Randolphs' corn crop. Photographer unknown. Courtesy Moon-Randolph Homestead.

expected to hear his slow voice on the line when I lifted the receiver of a wall phone.

Like his father, Bill was a tall, thin man and bore a striking resemblance to Abraham Lincoln. I remember watching him working his way up to the ridge in his old truck, hauling scrap iron to use in fence repair. Or I would see him strolling down to the barnyard to milk his goats, bucket swinging beside him, with a slow, duck-footed walk. His dog followed along while the goats bleated. The dogs were always collies, appropriately quiet and gentle like Bill. A patient and kind man, he was known to feed candy bars to his nanny goats. He went to town only rarely, but when returning he would honk his horn as he came up his dirt road. We'd hear a chorus of mooing and bleating as his animals welcomed him home. It is fitting that memorial gifts were to be sent to the Missoula Humane Society after his death.

I knew Bill only when he was a middle-aged and elderly man, but I felt a kinship with him. As an adolescent and teenager, I walked down to see him occasionally, crawling through the fence separating our places and skidding down the bank to his narrow dirt road. I'd bushwhack through native plums, box elder, and prickly rose bushes. I passed the unpainted barn with its worn brown siding and splotchy tin roof, salvaged from industrial cast-offs. Horse stalls and cattle pens lined the central, gambrel-roofed section with its hay loft above. Shed-roofed additions on each end added further to the patched-together look. Farther along, I peered into the winch shed at the old coal mine and ambled by the milk house, chicken house, and goat sheds, heading toward his little white house farther up the hill. It seemed so different on his side of the draw—more cozy, modest, and quiet. The orchard was always a mysterious, shady oasis, with its apple, sour cherry, pear, and crabapple trees huddled in the hollow. It was a little spooky too, with the disheveled carcasses of metal plows and other equipment half hidden in tall grass and the gnarled apple branches twisting for light. This woodsy part of the homestead was a magnet for wildlife, from nesting owls to browsing deer and the occasional raiding bear. I learned not to be scared as I passed the ramshackle buildings. Maybe the low tinkle of the goats' bells helped. I often carried baked goods or some scrawled message from my parents. Both introverts, Bill and I sat in his sparse kitchen while he patted the dog at his side. The conversations were short sentences with long pauses, but he seemed to like my visits.

Despite his eccentric, lonely ways, Bill wasn't a hermit. He worked the weekly cattle auction at the stockyards every Thursday for twenty-five years. For Bill, the stockyards provided an important supplement to his ranching income. The stockyards sprawled along the railroad tracks just west of the Missoula cemetery, only 2 miles from our houses. Bill took a sack lunch on Thursdays, walking when the road was drifted in with snow. My dad would often plow his road for him, but it drifted in deeply since his road followed the bottom of the draw.

Most sale days he drove his long black 1962 Chevy Impala. It had a red interior, quite snazzy for such a shy man. In my teenage years, my parents ran the café at the stockyards, and Bill loved my dad's homemade lemon meringue pie. He sat on a round, backless stool at the counter beside the cattle buyers, brand inspectors, and other farmers, quietly minding his own business with a cup of coffee and a piece of pie with its tall, stiff meringue. After we closed the café at the end of a sale day, we'd sometimes see Bill walking home and give him a lift up the hill.

Even though we lived close by, Bill's solitary nature created some distance. From my grandmother's diary entries, it is clear that my family socialized with the Randolphs more when Bill's parents were alive. Her 1946 diary has several entries about going down to the Randolphs' for a drink, riding horses to their place, and visiting with Emma. The neighborly connections in the North Hills ran deep. The Sunesons and Randolphs cut ice blocks together at Suneson's pond and hauled it to an ice house at the Randolphs'. The ice provided both ranches with refrigeration for several months. Even reclusive Bill seemed part of our extended family. He attended my wedding in 1972 and, three years later, served as a pallbearer at my grandmother's funeral.

Bill was born in 1911, four years after his parents purchased eighty acres in the hollow behind and northwest of Waterworks Hill for $1900. The Randolphs were the third owners of that land after Native American stewards. Although I knew Bill Randolph personally, I didn't know the older history of his land until reading Caitlin DeSilvey's *Butterflies and Railroad Ties: A History of a Montana Homestead* and talking with the author. DeSilvey documents how, in 1889, the same year Montana gained statehood, Ray Moon came to Missoula from Minnesota and followed an ephemeral creek up a draw to an open hillside that was fairly protected from the wind. He filed a homestead claim on 160 acres. During the requisite five years of proving up on the claim and obtaining a deed, Moon planted an orchard of seventy-five apple and cherry trees, built a small cabin, and cultivated more and more acreage for crops. Shortly after he obtained the deed to the land, he sold it to family members, who owned it until the Randolphs purchased the first eighty acres and then the other eighty-five years later.

They'd purchased marginal land, with dry, grassy foothills that seared in summer's heat and offered few amenities to homestead life in brutal winters. The North Hills were never the first choice for homesteading in the Missoula region; Grass Valley, west of town, was far more fertile. But settlers were hopeful. The land did offer possibilities for grazing and for growing crops if farmers could capture enough water. They needed stubbornness, cunning, and strong backs. Although the Randolph building cluster was less than two miles from downtown Missoula as the crow flies (and only about a half mile from the North Side neighborhood), they were completely out of sight or sound from town, situated in the far northwest corner of the property and tucked into the hill.

In the 1910s and 1920s, the Randolphs tried many income sources, including orchard crops and livestock. They sold milk, butter, and cream. William was quite a horseman and raised draft horses that he sold as teams. Born a Missourian before coming to Montana as a boy, he longed to be an inventor. His innovations, though never commercially successful, were a factor in developing the creative disorder that became the Randolph place. Although the early 1900s proved golden years for agriculture, with good prices and plentiful rainfall, the late teens and 1920s became economically difficult for farmers everywhere. The farm economy crashed in Montana. Homesteaders abandoned their efforts and went broke. Farmhouses stood empty. But the Randolphs held on by growing diverse cash crops and living frugally. The

YOU CAN'T EAT THE SCENERY / 57

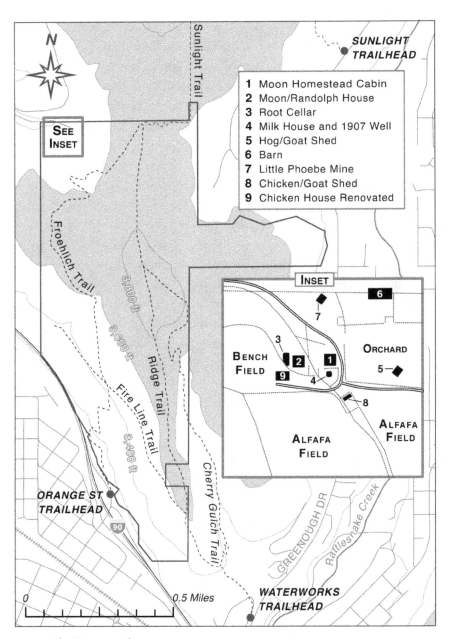

MAP 5. The Homestead

North Hills neighbors worked together, one of the keys to getting by. For instance, old diaries show that the Randolphs cooperated with the neighboring Suneson and Carlson families to put up hay.

William always thought he'd find gold in the North Hills. Instead he found coal. The Randolphs ran a small-scale coal-mining operation early in the century, even before buying their land in the North Hills. Old abstracts show that William leased land on the slopes west of Rattlesnake Creek in 1908 for coal mining. He paid $100 per year and ten cents per ton of coal sold. Then he developed a mine on his own land and named it the Little Phoebe. Through the 1920s it produced enough low-quality coal to keep several hired miners working in its shafts. After production at the Little Phoebe ended in 1937 and the mine shaft filled with water, the Randolphs pumped water from the mine to irrigate their vegetable garden. Today one wonders if that water was contaminated from mining.

Bill was the youngest of William's three boys. Their neighbor Coit Suneson was close in age to Bill's older brothers, Robert and Keith. I imagine the band of four exploring the secluded draws, trailing across the hillsides, and sledding down the roads in the 1910s and 1920s. Robert's 1916 diary mentions fun times with Coit, including birthday parties, skiing to school, making candy, sledding, and playing ball. He kept a running commentary on what the miners were up to in the coal mine.

The four boys walked or skied to school, following a trail they made over the hill toward Whittier School on Missoula's North Side. When blizzards prevented the walk home, the Randolph and Suneson parents told the boys to stay with a designated relative until it was safe to be out. Those arrangements were pre-arranged by the adults. My parents gave me the same instructions; as temperatures plummeted and snow blew sideways it was a treat to stay at my Aunt Betty's house on Howell Street, only two blocks from Lowell School.

North Hills farmers' self-sufficiency probably saved them during the Great Depression. They bartered, surviving in a nearly cashless economy. The Randolphs traded vegetables, eggs, pork, and coal for shoes, gas, medical services, and dry goods. Even some grocery stores bartered with farmers. Six days a week, William took a wagon and team of horses to town, peddling produce and dairy products. He sold beef from his Holstein steers, storing the meat in a cold, dark root cellar built into the hill and lined on one side with meat hooks. A seasonal rhythm guided this hard work. By the 1930s the Randolphs, like their neighbor Jonas Suneson, had a steady base of household and commercial accounts. In Missoula, as elsewhere during the Depression, townsfolk bought their produce from farmers like the Randolphs and Sunesons, or from small local outlets that purchased directly from those farmers. Urban residents depended on nearby farmers. Emma Randolph's stationery advertised her chickens: "Mrs. W.H. Randolph, Eggs for hatching from finest strain, White leghorn chickens, Ranch located two miles north of city, Missoula, Montana." The Randolphs sold lettuce, turnip greens, and peas early in the spring and then ran a "you-pick" operation for pie cherries later in the summer.

The Randolphs' ranch swelled to 414 acres by 1939, including much of the south-facing hillside overlooking downtown Missoula. Throughout the 1940s, the Randolphs increased their operations with dairy, beekeeping, beef cattle, and a market garden. Like my grandmother, Emma Randolph optimistically planted a hedge of caragana and currants to create a yard, trying to tame and beautify the bare hillsides. The visits between Emma Randolph and Selma Suneson, and later my grandma, Mildred Kramen, were probably fueled by the women's plans for cultivating their dooryards with flowers and shrubs.

As those hedges grew taller, farming and ranching changed dramatically. By the 1950s and 1960s most farmers and ranchers in Missoula County had consolidated lands into large stock or dry land grain operations. During the Eisenhower era, many Americans prospered as never before. As the standard of living for the beneficiaries of this prosperity boom exceeded what previous generations had only dreamed of, small-scale subsistence farming, like the Randolph homestead, became obsolete. Nationwide the number of farms, farmers and rural residents declined. Specialization increased dramatically as farms became larger and consumers bought their food from grocery stores, not from local farmers.

William and Emma Randolph expanded the ranch to 585 acres in the early 1950s, but otherwise their homestead remained relatively unchanged. Both died in 1956, leaving Bill to work the ranch. His brothers had left by then for other occupations. Bill expanded the goat herd after his parents' death. He tried to keep the place from falling apart, put up a little hay, and occasionally sold livestock. He boarded horses on his hillsides for Missoula residents. This, in addition to his work at the stockyards, became a primary source of income. In Bill's later years, my parents helped him put up hay with their machinery, a job he had always done with a team of horses; none of the Randolphs ever owned a tractor. In most respects he was out of sync with the community his land bordered.

Missoula's Peace Sign, located on Randolph property facing Missoula, was a blatant symbol of discord between Missoula and the North Hills. For over twenty years, through the 1980s and 1990s, a loose band of secretive Missoula activists painted the round symbol on an outdated microwave reflecting tower. Repeatedly, they worked under cover of night to paint the twenty-five-by-thirty-foot surface. The owner, a communications company that leased a small plot of land from Bill Randolph, painted over the peace sign many times, creating a visible community tug-of-war. Occasionally, people from all over downtown Missoula would wake up in the morning and find the peace sign restored. Missoula residents were divided about this particular symbol. Many people loved its tranquil message overlooking the city, while others discredited it as a hippie affront to Vietnam veterans. Because the peace symbol was an invention of Vietnam War protesters and the counterculture of the 1960s, Bill Randolph disliked its standing on his land, as did other North Hills ranchers. My mother was ashamed of the peace sign as an emblem of the North Hills. She's glad it's now gone. In a typical generational split, I—on the other hand—loved seeing it there.

In 2001 the tower's owner dismantled the peace sign, but a grassroots rescue mission salvaged it. Bob Oakes, a community organizer, gave nine eight-by-ten-foot panels to "caretakers" across Missoula, who display them in their yards. He defined guardianship: "The pieces cannot be sold. They cannot be given away without notifying the folks of their whereabouts. They can't be painted over. And if the pieces decide that they need to come back together someday, you have to give your piece back." Some of the pieces are riddled with bullet holes and stained from slurry bombing dumps during the July 2000 wildfire in the North Hills. Bill did not live long enough to see it pulled from his hillside.

Bill remained a bachelor his entire life. By the 1990s his place was, in most respects, still the homestead that Ray Moon and Bill's parents had created more than eighty years earlier. All but Bill's house, remodeled in 1946 from an outbuilding, are relics of the original Moon homestead. Bill wanted to keep it that way. It is somewhat ironic that such a reticent man became a conservation pioneer in the Missoula area. Before he died, he placed a conservation easement on his land, one of the first landowners to do so on a large piece of land near town. A conservation easement permanently limits development of private land. It is a legal agreement between a landowner and a nonprofit land trust or government agency that protects wildlife habitat, open space, and other values. Landowners who put easements on their land continue to own and use the land and may sell it, lease it, or pass it on to their heirs, but any owners must follow the easement terms.

Bill worked with Five Valleys Land Trust in Missoula to place the easement on over half of his land in December 1992, three years before his death. The easement aimed to "preserve and protect in perpetuity and to enhance and restore the open space, historic and natural features and values of the property." Bill sought to prevent his land from being developed after he was gone. Once he signed the legal paperwork at the courthouse, he walked with a couple of the land trust's board and staff members to a little café close by. Late in life, Bill had become quite deaf, so the conversation was probably difficult. Happy to have made an important step for his land, I'm told he celebrated by ordering cherry pie.

Bill's conservation easement made the front page of the *Missoulian*, and my mom sent the clipping to me in Ann Arbor. The land remained Bill's point of reference until the end. On his death bed he told my mother he was "going to the marble orchard." When he died in 1995, his land had been cultivated for a century. He spent his last days in St. Patrick Hospital, where my cousin Richard worked as a night-shift nurse. Coincidentally Richard had worked with Bill at the stockyards years before. Bill was comfortable sharing stories late at night in the ward's quiet darkness, free of distractions. Bill's window on the top floor faced north. He could see the sun rise over Mount Jumbo and see the soft morning light glowing on the public-facing side of his ranch. He was satisfied it would remain intact.

I took both a personal and professional interest in Bill's decision since I was teaching and conducting research on rural land conservation at the University of Michigan. Once I moved back to Missoula a dozen years later, I worked with land trusts to achieve more of what Bill had envisioned on rural lands across the west. Bill and I continued to have a connection rooted in the North Hills.

The City of Missoula purchased Bill's land in 1996, using open space bond funding the voters had approved in 1995, the year Bill died. This was the beginning of Missoula's focus on conserving the North Hills landscape and kicked off significant public involvement aimed at planning the homestead's future. The North Side Missoula Community Development Corporation, started in 1996, sponsored a 1998 campaign to preserve the homestead, creating the Hill and Homestead Preservation to work on preserving the historic homestead and to document its history.

The Randolph place became iconic for many Missoulians. It is now called "the Moon-Randolph Homestead," and the public can hike the hills, pick apples in the orchard, and learn about tending chickens. A series of caretakers has lived in Bill's house, in each case cherishing the special ambiance of the homestead, even though they must haul drinking water from town. In 2010 the National Park Service placed the Homestead on the National Register of Historic Places, deeming it historic "at the local level of significance, for its association with broad patterns in Missoula valley settlement and agricultural history."

The Randolph family's legacy became public as the managers of the homestead revealed diaries found in Bill's house, examined his decaying outbuildings, and documented the contents of the root cellar. I've often wondered what Bill would think about all this. In 1998 the Missoulian published, word-for-word, Robert Randolph's diary from 1917, the year he was thirteen. Bill was protecting the ground, blissfully unaware that his family's life would become public.

PHOTO 7. Hoar frost scene at the Moon-Randolph Homestead. Photo by Harriet Spurlock. Author's family collection.

Today, Missoula residents value the North Hills, not for the pie cherries, beef, or eggs making their way to city plates, but for scenery, history, recreation, and habitat—in short, for its setting and landscape. It is also valued for the physical artifacts of a way of life. Even without human presence, the farmstead has the imprint of the family who lived there so long. The variety of outbuildings is evidence of subsistence in a challenging landscape. The creative use of car frames and plow parts utilized for fencing shows the family's ingenuity. Theodore Roosevelt wrote, "Do what you can, with what you have, where you are." The Randolphs complied.

Buildings were patched together, were added onto, and became rundown. The simple nostalgia of this slow decay is a magnet in our modern world. People are fascinated by leaning outbuildings sided with photogenic old tin signs, random weathered boards, and patchworks of rusty license plates. The wooden walls of the milk house were salvaged from old boxcar siding: recycled boxcars would later feature prominently in the North Hills. There is a quaint beauty in gates made from old metal headboards and fence posts fashioned from shovels, bedsprings, or rooted tree trunks. The Randolphs planted an upended rusty car chassis in a fence line at the top of Randolph Hill. The Moon-Randolph Homestead was featured in a 2010 *Sunset* magazine article by Caroline Patterson, its rusted tin-roof barn visible in the photos of the homesteading caretakers.

But the deeper meanings—slowness, ingenuity, and collaboration—are even more important. Schoolkids now learn about gardening and raising chickens, and Missoulians are re-discovering the value of local food through programs at the homestead. The early pioneers, and even modern-day North Hills residents, believe that what comes off the land is what matters most. They brought fresh food—butter, apples, potatoes, and more—from the hills to sell in town. Native bunchgrasses sustained cattle, sheep, and other livestock. The ranches nourished the families who settled there, as well as their neighbors in town. The special sense of community between North Hills ranchers and their town neighbors was slowly eroded over many decades, but it is being reinvigorated by programs at the homestead.

Older generations of North Hills residents are saddened by what little comes off these places now. My mom cares more about the products these places yield than the recreational opportunities or scenic views that urban neighbors covet. Perhaps the hodgepodge of the Randolph place can show us that the two sets of values can be melded, that the North Hills *can* grow things while also providing cultural amenities. The absence of houses is not enough to ensure that these hills benefit the growing city. Maybe the North Hills can once again provide commodities for Missoula's urban population. Bill Randolph's whirligig—a tiny energy solution—symbolizes the kind of local, small-scale problem-solving that was always there and will be needed in the future.

5

LAND RICH, CASH POOR

The older generation had greater respect for land than science. But we live in an age when science, more than soil, has become the provider of growth and abundance. Living just on the land creates loneliness in an age of globality.
—Shimon Peres, *The Guardian*, 2011

The weather spits, then shines, then grays. It's an unsettled, dismal day, fitting for this Halloween day of 2009. I drive up Coal Mine Road, past the landfill entrance, over a dilapidated cattle guard, to Archie Carlson's cinderblock house. A wooden coal bin is the biggest visible structure, leaning toward the hill near Archie's house. For me, one charm of the Carlson place is that its backdrop is the timbered ridge of our Big Pasture, not visible from our ranch buildings due to hilly topography. I pull into a yard strewn with vehicles in various states of disrepair. The process of small-scale, marginal enterprise leaves debris, often visible and still deteriorating generations later.

I reach into the back seat for the bag of bagels and a cooked turkey breast I've brought for Archie and make my way to his house. I find him sitting on a pile of tires near his front door puffing on a cigarette. He's wearing old jeans, work boots, a stained baseball cap, and an insulated plaid work shirt. Archie is a gaunt seventy-one year old with a long, angular face, narrow mustache, and piercing eyes that reveal an ardent, wild intelligence. Seriously ill from a lifetime of smoking, he looks many years older. But, as usual, he is friendly and upbeat, despite persistent pain. His drawl could easily be Oklahoman, acquired from his mother, Nora, who was a native of that state. My mom remembers that the first time she went to the Carlsons' house as a young girl, she was amazed that Nora was frying green tomatoes.

Other than a few army years in the mid-1960s, Archie has spent his entire life at this ranch. He never married and lived with Nora in this modest single-story house, once white and now a blurry gray. Since Nora's death at ninety-two in 2002, he's been alone. The house is a few hundred yards east of the much older two-story brick ranch house where his brother Walt lives. They jointly own this ranch with sister Mildred, who lives in eastern Montana.

Archie seems pleased to see me. When I ask how he's doing, he says, "Been having trouble with my digestive tract; can't eat much. It just goes through me." This is a typical Archie accounting of various bodily functions, always more information than one really wants. He has been working today on a faded blue 1987 Chevy Blazer, up on blocks a mere six feet from his door. "Blocks" is an overstatement. The tires teeter on a narrow pile of lumber—two-by-fours and other odd pieces that look like they've been there a very long time. He explains that he hurt his shoulder working on the rig's transmission and is now having trouble reaching under the hood to pour in a few quarts of oil. Archie heels his cigarette into the ground and then shows me into the house, apologizing that he hasn't felt well enough to clean the place. I walk through the kitchen, which shows few signs of cooking, past the wood range that heats the house. He hasn't fired it yet today, so I keep my coat on. Past the kitchen, I head into the connected living and dining areas, which are filled with piles of papers, computer carcasses, mechanic's tools, and neatly folded laundry. Archie proudly shows me the patches he sewed on a very worn flannel shirt last night—tidy, almost invisible handmade stitches. In the big, streaky south-facing window, a dusty Christmas cactus perches on the sill and a pair of binoculars balances on a tripod, trained on the road leading up to the house and down over the Missoula valley.

I'VE COME TO TALK to Archie about his family's history in the North Hills. I've known Archie my whole life, but over the last thirty years I have seen him only occasionally. I want to glean his experience of being a North Hills rancher in the twenty-first century and his family's history on this land. I am particularly curious about local coal mining, stories he knows in surprising detail given that they predate his birth. A dark obsolete coal mine seems an appropriately spooky topic today. Coal miners dug at the Carlson place for nearly sixty years, starting in the 1880s and ending in 1942, a year before Archie was born. "My dad and uncle John told me the mining history lotsa times," he explains.

"The mine tunnels caved in, in the 1950s. Termites chewed the beams." Archie points outside to a slight rise not far from the house. There's really nothing visible of the mine itself, but he explains that miners dug a thousand-foot tunnel into the hillside, with two shifts of twelve men working the mine daily, between 1920 and 1940. They excavated forty or fifty lateral tunnels to access the coal seam, whose origin goes back forty million years. "All the blasting was done with black powder about the size of raisins." Archie chuckles. The mine yielded poor-quality but salable coal. He says, "You carried two buckets of coal into the house and one bucket of ash out. On a bad day it was the other way around—one bucket of coal in and two buckets of ash out." Miners moved coal out of the mine in wooden carts that rolled on a track. They hoisted a string of cars up out of the mine with different sources of power over sixty years—horses, a Studebaker engine, steam power. When Archie points outside, I can see the hulk of a coal car decaying in the field.

Archie pulls a framed eight-by-ten sepia-colored photo from a shelf. "That was taken in about 1940 and that's my dad there." Carl Carlson stands on a wagon of loose hay, a team of horses hitched to it. Cows gather to feed in the foreground. But Archie wants me to see what's behind the wagon and cows—the coal bin. "That bin was built in 1888, stood about sixty feet tall and oh, probably forty feet wide." It looms in front of a mound of mine waste—what Archie calls the muck pile—nearly as high as the coal bin. Miners used the muck pile as a ramp, pulling coal cars up it then dumping coal into sorting chutes at the top of the bin itself. When it was time to sell coal, they loaded it onto wagons, and later trucks, then through another set of chutes with doors on the downhill side. I step to the front window, where I see the coal bin, downslope and to the side of Archie's house, a ghostly relic of the ranch's coal-mining era. Later, when I photograph it, Archie wants to pose in front, clearly proud of that legacy. The Carlsons hauled hundreds of loads of muck to downtown Missoula, where they sold it for fill. Muck, as it turns out, was yet another product hauled from the North Hills to Missoula. The muck pile still helps support some prominent downtown Missoula buildings.

When I ask about the string of ownership on his place, Archie fetches the ranch's abstract from his basement. It's a yellowed bundle of legal-sized papers an inch thick, stapled across the top, the earliest transactions on top. It details the homestead claim John Richli made on 160 acres in 1890, nearly the same time that homesteaders settled the other two North Hills places.

President Grover Cleveland signed Richli's deed from the U.S. government in 1895 once he'd proved up. The Northern Pacific tracks reached Missoula in 1883, the same year Missoula incorporated, giving Richli a ready market for his coal.

The abstract's dusty pages bring the place to life. Archie explains, "You'll see in there that the Missoula Coal Mine sat on five acres owned separate from the 160-acre homestead. It had the miners' bunkhouse, the mine entrance, the coal bin, and a mine boss's cabin." The abstract shows each ownership change, including purchases, tax delinquencies, and all other legal transactions affecting the deed. Abstracts are usually complicated and confusing, partly because of the different types of land rights that one can own—water rights, mineral rights, access easements. I browse through the sheaf of papers and find a few key names and dates, all of them consistent with Archie's story.

70 / THREE RANCHES ON THE EDGE

PHOTO 8. Archie Carlson leaning on the old coal bin at Hellgate Ranch in 2006. Photo by Donna Erickson.

Richli obtained water rights on the mine site, and water would become an important part of the coal mine story.

Archie's grandfather Gustav Carlson bought Richli's homestead in 1911, the same year the Randolphs came to the North Hills. Archie says, "When my grandfather saw this place, he thought it would be a good place to grow potatoes and to raise cows." He named the place Hellgate Ranch, and successive generations of Carlsons have lived here for a hundred years. The name Hellgate refers to Hellgate Canyon, between Mount Sentinel and Mount Jumbo, on Missoula's eastern edge. The Flathead and Blackfeet used the steep, narrow canyon to battle one another on the Road to the Buffalo. The canyon had so many exposed human bones that French fur trappers later called it the "Gates of Hell."

Gustav arrived in the U.S. by ship, as a teenager, in 1882 from an early life of fishing on the North Sea. He and his wife Christina, also a Swedish immigrant, bore two sons—Carl in 1905 and John in 1909. The boys attended Whittier School on the North Side with Coit Suneson and the Randolph brothers. In 1918 the flu pandemic hit Missoula. Between 3 and 5 percent of the world's population died, with some places hit harder than others. Half of the children in Carl's and John's classes died. Gustav and Christina pulled their boys out of school, so Carl stopped at the eighth grade and John at only fourth.

Archie starts to tell me more about his grandparents' enterprises but stops and declares it "too damn cold in here." He decides to start a fire in the old Monarch cookstove, which he says his parents bought in the 1930s. "I got this weed burner I use here, makes one helluva fire." A small propane tank sits in the middle of the kitchen, attached to the weed burner with its long handle and metal torch at the end. Archie opens the valve on the propane and sticks the torch in the firebox. I hear a whooshing sound as he fires it up for a few minutes, igniting the chunks of pine lumber in the firebox. "This thing really keeps the stovepipe cleaned out!" This whole scenario is frightening, given that the oxygen tank for Archie's respirator sits about five feet away. After the fire starts crackling, we return to the living room and Archie continues.

"My granddad bought work horses, started a cattle operation, and planted an orchard with forty apple and plum trees. I used to eat apples off those trees. Some years the worms would survive the winter and the apples weren't so good, but some years there were no worms." The orchard produced well into the 1950s, but the Carlsons then left it to the worms. Bears climbed the trees and broke the limbs; the entrepreneurial Carlsons then sold applewood for smoking fish, and eventually the orchard dwindled to nothing. Like the Randolphs, the Carlsons sold fruits and vegetables in Missoula, maintaining wholesale accounts with Worden's Market and the Missoula Mercantile in the oldest part of town. They grew potatoes to sell, storing three to four tons each winter in a cellar under the original brick farmhouse.

After getting his cattle operation launched, Gustav bought the mine site in 1930 for back taxes, renaming it Hellgate Mine. The abstract shows he paid $2.48. The Carlsons always hired mining contractors to run the mines and keep crews employed. "They'd get people off the street, usually from Murphy's Corner, and teach 'em how to do the work. Men lived here in a bunkhouse so they wouldn't be going to town and hauling off shovels and pick axes." Archie later grew up in that bunkhouse, abandoned now but still standing, after the mines closed and before Carl built the cinder-block house in 1956.

Another dilapidated cabin, which housed the mine boss, also sits near the coal bin. Archie tells me a tale from those times, showing the wild-west nature of the business. "The mine manager at that old mine hadn't paid his workers. They threatened to hang him and were getting a noose ready when my granddad stepped in with a rifle and told them they could hang him but they weren't going to do it on his place." He saved the man's life and loaned him the money to pay the wages. In typical Montana form, Archie just relays these startling facts without real emotion, apart from some pride in his grandfather's heroism.

Archie retains numbers. I glaze over at the many numbers he spits out; he explains that they pumped six hundred gallons of alkaline water per hour—with a steam engine, through a four-inch pipe, twenty-four-hours a day—to keep the main mine from filling. "Miners had to wear raincoats all year. It was always dripping and muddy down there." Water, in these dry North Hills, was probably more important than the coal income. A windmill still stands above the mine, installed after coal mining stopped. It pumped water to irrigate potatoes and fill cattle tanks. He never went into the dangerous mine tunnels as a child because they were filled with water. The Carlsons not only irrigated their own crops with the mine water, but also piped it to potato fields on a farm south of theirs. In the 1960s, when construction crews built Interstate 90 across the edge of Missoula and across the southern edge of the Carlson place, they used water from the mines for mixing concrete. Archie starts with the numbers again: "They pumped about one thousand gallons per hour and worked it continually over two and a half months—a million gallons a month. Lowered the mine's water level only two and a half feet." When I ask Archie why they stopped mining, he explains that "the war was going on in Germany and brass was getting in short supply and we needed brass for the pumping. And the price of coal started to go to hell."

In Gustav's time, brick-making added another income. He mined clay from a pit about a quarter of a mile uphill from his barn. Like local coal, Missoula bricks were low quality—soft and porous. But digging clay remained commercially viable for some time. Carlson hauled clay to Standard Lime and Brick, a small brick kiln at the base of the North Hills near the Missoula cemetery. Bricks from that kiln helped form Higgins Avenue, Missoula's main street. Archie explains that "on a day in May of 1930, my granddad started down the road with a horse and wagon, hauling one and a half tons of clay across a shallow draw. The clay was for lining a furnace at a foundry in town. His horses spooked at a bear and my granddad landed in a diversion ditch. He broke his neck and died a couple of days later." Again, I'm surprised that he relays this story with a matter-of-fact accounting, partly because the incident happened long before he was born. He did not know his grandfather.

After Gustav died, Carl and John took over, running shorthorn cattle and a few longhorns. In 1939 they bought 320 acres adjoining the original homestead to the south. When I mention my surprise at the brothers being able to make that purchase at the end of the Great Depression, Archie explains that the county was selling it for delinquent taxes. "My dad and uncle went down to see about buying that land. A county commissioner wanted some of it himself, but of course couldn't bid on it. He agreed that if Dad and Uncle John would split some of it off to sell to him, he'd loan them the money to buy it." This clearly smacks of political impropriety, but the Carlsons wanted the land so they could graze their cattle closer to home. "My dad was running about two hundred head of cattle and leasing pasture way up the Clark Fork. They'd move them cows over Waterworks Hill, dog the hell out of 'em down in Cherry Gulch, around Mount Jumbo, out to East Missoula, and up the river to Nimrod."

The property they bought extends to the edge of Missoula's North Side neighborhood and abuts the Randolph land on the east. This is the Carlson land I know the best, as the road to our place passes through it and I walked across it almost every day as a child in the 1960s. My mom or dad often drove me to Lowell School, but I usually walked home over the viaduct spanning the railroad tracks, through the North Side neighborhood, along the county road past the cemetery, through the Carlsons' pastureland, and up the steep hill to our house—about two and a half miles. It took me an hour or more to get home, and I particularly disliked the section through the Carlsons'. Its wide, open hillsides gave no protection from heat, cold, or wind—or from the Carlsons' grazing cattle. I worried I'd be trampled, since their bulls threatened me a couple of times. I felt more comfortable on horseback when it came to other peoples' cattle. By the time I was twelve, I rode a red moped to school, not much more than a bike with a lawn mower motor. A homeowner near the viaduct let me store it in his garage each morning. Then I'd walk over the viaduct to school and retrieve it again at the end of the school day for the easy, though illegal, ride home.

The landfill, across the Randolph fence line, adds an ominous feel to the place. The actual dump pit rotates across the landfill property as one area is filled and covered and the bulldozers dig new pits. My mom told me, "I remember going to a meeting at the White Pine about putting the landfill in the North Hills. Archie gave a long, articulate speech protesting the landfill next to his land." But this was the ultimate NIMBY—Not in My Backyard—complaint, which minimized the credibility of his argument. As I drove up today, I noticed that the dump plunges northward, closer and closer to the Carlsons. Blowing plastic bags form white drifts inside the ten-foot industrial chain link fence separating Carlson land from the landfill. Hundreds of two-

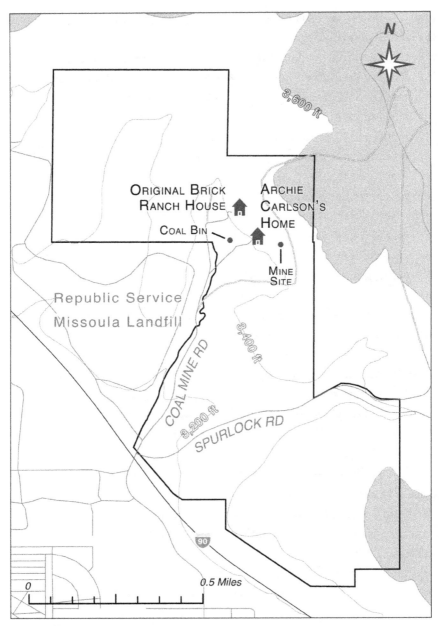

MAP 6. Hellgate Ranch

foot-long ravens circle overhead. The shiny black-blue birds, with wingspans over four feet, create a sinister mood for Halloween, and I duck my head instinctively as a conspiracy of ravens swoops over the car. When I mention the dump to Archie, he's resigned after all these years, claiming that "they are pretty good neighbors," and turns the conversation toward the bulldozers' horsepower—he has those numbers down pat.

Archie's acumen with all things mechanical reminds me that things are more industrial at their place than at ours or the Randolphs'. The mining legacy and the landfill are only part of it. Our ranch activity revolved around horses and cattle, and even though that meant keeping vehicles in running order—horse trailers, trucks, haying equipment—we weren't as focused on machinery and motors as the Carlsons. I never saw them herding cattle on horseback; they were more apt to do it on a motorbike. When my parents wanted to build the road that circles the east side of the Big Pasture, it was Walt Carlson they called, who pushed that road through on his old D-8 Caterpillar. When I ask Archie if he ever rode horses growing up, he explains that they mostly had draft horses. "We used horse-drawn mowers and rakes until 1954." In general, I think my family was more in love with the romance of ranching than the Carlsons were.

After the brothers died—Carl in 1969 and John in 1971—the ranch passed to Carl's three offspring, who own it now. As Archie and I talk, he makes oblique references to the brick house where his brother Walt lives. There is no trail between the two houses; the two brothers live only a few hundred yards apart and have not spoken to one another since disputes about their Uncle John's estate. For over forty years Archie and Walt have not spoken. They do not jointly manage day-to-day decisions about the ranch, much less plan its future. In the 1980s, when we drove to the Carlsons at night, we'd see hundreds of eyes shining in the dark. Walt bought rabbits and let them multiply into the hundreds, specifically to thwart gardening at Archie's place.

Now the land is valuable, possibly for expansion of the landfill, but also for housing or other uses. So, like Skyline Ranch, Hellgate Ranch lies in limbo. Being up here feels like holding a long exhale, waiting for the next

LAND RICH, CASH POOR / 77

breath of life. While the land's mining chapter is surely over, it can still support cattle. But Archie barely ekes out a living with his few shorthorn cows. He struggles to buy enough hay to winter them over; in summer his cows are mysteriously fat, given that the land is severely overgrazed. We joke that they seem to survive on rocks and weeds. His place could likely grow houses more productively, although that might be feasible only after the landfill owners have reclaimed the land or moved on to another part of their property.

Despite struggles *within* families, many of them over land, the three families of the North Hills cooperated and got along for most of the twentieth century and well into the twenty-first. They worked at neighborly fence upkeep, coaxed the county to plow drifted roads, and, of course, complained about the weather. At one time or another they've leased land from one another, borrowed each other's equipment, and hauled home wayward cattle from neighbors' corrals. My mom remembers that when she was maybe ten years old, she walked a milk cow over to the Carlsons' to be bred with their bull. When I ask about these relationships, Archie says, "Oh you know my family always got along just fine with your grandparents and you all . . . Randolphs too." I know this is not entirely true. We have the copy of a letter my grandfather's attorney sent to the Carlsons insisting they not step foot on Skyline Ranch again. Apparently, as teenagers, Walt and Archie were shooting at water tanks and getting into other mischief.

My mother relies on Archie, knowing he'd help out at a moment's notice in any emergency. He is a good neighbor, reliable and honest. And he appreciates that we were always the eyes and ears on the side of his place where our road passed through. My mom still occasionally calls Archie after a trip to town, telling him she saw a cow down, straining to calve, or someone dumping their garbage on his land after the landfill closed for the day.

A confluence of life stories kept a few hardy homesteaders and their offspring on these hillsides, and now Archie and my mom get by on their places, past the extraction era. Like many Montanans, they are land rich and cash poor—just getting by on land with tremendous value. In some parts of the state, oil and gas lie below the surface; in the North Hills the value stems from two incompatible uses—habitat for people, on the one hand, and habitat for elk on the other. And, at least in the Carlsons' case, putting stuff into the ground—garbage—is potentially a far more lucrative endeavor than taking coal or clay out. It is ironic that three generations of Carlsons grubbed a living literally out of the ground, and now the land is worth millions of dollars for other reasons.

As Archie and I wrap up our afternoon together, topics range from maps to motorcycles to megabytes, and he has numeric data on each topic. The subject somehow turns to milk. Archie retrieves a book from his bedroom, in order to convince me that milk may not be good for adults. It is a three-inch-thick biochemistry textbook, and Archie remembers that the two paragraphs on lactose intolerance are on page 571. It reminds him to tell me more about his digestive system and about milking cows on Hellgate Ranch. This is the usual wandering of a conversation with Archie—ranging back and forth in time and across myriad details but always coming back to the ranch. He tells me that "after fifty you get some wisdom and think about all you've done and what you could have done better." Then he grins widely and adds, "my best memories are riding my Kawasaki motorcycle." He's been a motor-head all along. On the way to my car, Archie supervises as I pour six quarts of motor oil into his blue Blazer.

PART 2

STORIES FROM THE EDGE

6

I PLEDGE MY HEAD TO CLEARER THINKING

I pledge my Head to clearer thinking, my Heart to greater loyalty, my Hands to larger service and my Health to better living, for my club, my community, my country, and my world.

—The 4-H Pledge

Not the first day of school. Not the last. From the ages of nine to nineteen the landmark day in my year was the Tuesday before the Missoula County Fair started. I'm fourteen years old and riding in the back of the red Ford pickup as my dad drives South Avenue toward the fairgrounds. I notice creamy clouds in deep blue skies. I cling to the metal stock rack with both hands, steadying my red tack box at my feet, refreshed by the warm air floating by, my long brown hair flying. I've used stencils to paint my name and club name—*Ridge Runners*—in big white letters on the front below the 4-H clover. The box contains my gear—clippers and a wool carder, a feed pan, and my white shirt for the show ring, carefully folded in plastic.

My two sheep—a breeding ewe and a fattened lamb—balance next to me on unsteady legs, far more used to the grassy hillsides of our ranch in Missoula's North Hills. My horse, Blue, is alert and steady in the horse trailer behind, with Skyline Jack, a tall Appaloosa gelding, beside her. I've started showing them at horse shows around western Montana, so they are accustomed to trailer rides.

As we pass Sentinel High School, the fairgrounds come into view—a scene that's fresh and bright in my mind fifty years later. The Ferris wheel spins slowly as the roustabouts wrench machinery in place for the carnival rides. A John Deere drags its harrow around the racetrack, smoothing the sandy dirt for tomorrow's opening of the horse racing schedule. A water tanker follows, spraying the surface to keep dust down. Cars, trucks, and pickups navigate through the big fair gateway, delivering exhibits and livestock. For 1967 Missoula, this is heavy traffic. Vehicles brim with vegetables, shocks of wheat, hand-stitched quilts, and other homemade and homegrown treasures. We turn off South Avenue into the fairgrounds. Bright plastic flags flutter in long lines, pointing people in the right direction. Just in front of us, a truck pulls a small white trailer, I C E printed in big red letters with a white and blue snow cap topping each letter.

The fair always inspires excitement, community bonding, and pride, but this year will bring a tragedy that bonds Missoulians around loss. The region is hot and dry in late August; the needle on the fire danger thermometer points to EXTREME. We haven't had rain since June. As we turn east toward the horse barns, the big rainbird sprinklers spray the grass with a *sha-shink— sha-shink*. The maintenance men are still greening up the forty-acre grounds for the main event of the summer. We deliver Blue and Jack to the first stately barn closest to the fairground entrance. These first two barns are old and roomy. They allow show horses to live in relative luxury, compared with the low, musty racehorse stables, with their shed roofs and peeling paint, at the back side of the racetrack. After feeding and watering the horses, we drive to the other side of the fairgrounds.

The office near the main turnstile teems with people—including Coca Cola vendors, rodeo announcers, livestock judges, and racehorse owners. Golf carts pull little wagons loaded with weed whips, extra trash bins, petunia pots, and "No Parking" signs. Past the office, we take the small road around the two big exhibit buildings that anchor the Missoula County Fairgrounds. Ole Bakke, an influential Missoula architect of the early twentieth century, designed the one nearest the entrance and named it the Agricultural Palace. With its graceful rooflines, twin cupolas on top, and arched gable windows, the building showcases community pride and rural heritage. For the rest of the year, these buildings seem deserted, but they come into their own as centerpieces of the fair.

Traversing the fair's narrow internal streets—Race Way, Stakes Street, Carnival Way—we pass smaller, more modest buildings. Each has its name painted on a board above the door—Floriculture, Home Arts, Horticulture. The county moved two low-slung wood-frame buildings to the fairgrounds in 1955 from Fort Missoula, where they housed Civilian Conservation Corp workers and then Italian immigrants interned during World War II. I crane my neck to see what Missoula townsfolk are dropping off—pristine gladiolas, golden pies, and jewel-toned jellies. Dust swirls around a truck where a man is unloading a pumpkin three feet in diameter.

We head for my real fair home—the sheep barn. It fits snugly between the hog barn and the 4-H show ring, with its sawdust-covered arena open to the sky and sides ringed with small wooden bleachers. Small sheep pens— big enough for only one or two sheep—march down each side of two long walking aisles. In a plywood loft, which runs the length of the wall above the sheep, kids stash their hay, grain, buckets, and personal gear. I set my tack box up in the Ridge Runners section of the loft, which also makes a good napping spot. It's like settling in at summer camp, but better. The barn smells of clean straw, lanolin, and sweet alfalfa hay.

Each fall, 4-H members choose one or more projects—topics to explore for a year. 4-H offers a menu of nearly two hundred projects, from which kids

I PLEDGE MY HEAD TO CLEARER THINKING / 85

choose based on interests, cost, and ability. 4-Hers then complete activities related to the project area, keep records of progress, give oral presentations, and enter competitions, all with the mentoring of parents and 4-H leaders. I learned to develop film in photography, prevent wildfires in forestry, and baste pleats in sewing. Now I have two days to finish getting my fattened lamb, a Hampshire wether (castrated ram) born March 2, ready to show. I launched an oats-feeding regime and for six months kept meticulous records of his increasing weight and every expense in raising him. I lost $2.01 my first year in the sheep business, but I made steadily higher profits over the next five years.

Our home ranch seemed vast to me, although it was not as large or lush as the ranches out in the big western Montana valleys. But land tenure didn't matter at the fair. The fair was an equalizer. If I prepared and presented my animals well, I had as good a chance as anyone at succeeding. The trappings so visible at horse shows or races—fancy horse trailers, expensive saddles— were not central to the scene here. This was about the kids and their projects. And the show ring was hallowed ground. Anything was possible in that pavilion, with its fragrant blond shavings.

On show morning, the bleachers are full of parents perched in anticipation. The judge, sweating already in his starched white shirt and bolo tie, stands wide-legged in the middle of the ring holding his clipboard as fifteen kids lead sheep in a wide circle. We don't use ropes or halters on the one-hundred-pound animals but simply guide them with one hand under the chin and the other on the rump if needed. I wait, keeping my lamb's hooves planted in a perfect square, as the judge looks over the animals to my right. I'm next. He probes my lamb's thighs, rib cage, and backbone. I shift my location, *always* keeping my eyes on the judge and *never* coming between him and the lamb. After a half hour, he has studied all the lambs, scribbled on his clipboard, and walked to the microphone on the judge's stand to announce his ratings.

The judge's helper asks me and four others to pull our sheep forward from the line. He hands blue ribbons to the five of us, and then one girl is motioned farther forward to accept the coveted purple Grand Champion ribbon. Even though everyone wins a ribbon—blue for first place, red for second, or white for third—we all covet the blue and only dream of getting the singular purple ribbon.

The following morning I show Blue in an arena near the horse barns, and my parents show Jack in the afternoon. I ride Blue with my western saddle with braided rawhide reins, wearing my handmade western outfit. 4-H was a place where I could excel in my own way, be recognized, and accept responsibility. It taught me to get along with other people, set goals, make decisions, and determine my passions. Healthy competition was a part of it, backed up with a sense of competence and fairness.

The fair is starting to wind down. The number of details involved in transporting, housing, and showing livestock at a large fair is mind-boggling. This year, my exhausted parents decide to move home from the fair in stages. They begin with the horses, hauling them home on Wednesday evening when their show events are complete.

The traditional fireworks ended each day of the Missoula County Fair. That night after dark—10:00 p.m. or so in August—the fair day culminated in fireworks exploding from the infield at the close of the grandstand show. My family and I joined in the "ooos" and "aahhs" of the crowd of hundreds as the colors exploded over our heads. But the show sparked a far worse end.

At about 4:00 a.m. the following morning, Thursday, August 24, 1967, the barn where Blue and Jack had lounged only hours before burned to the ground. The fire also destroyed another barn nearby. Twenty-six horses died. Missoula's fire chief insisted that fireworks were not to blame, but Missoulians always suspected otherwise and the cause was never confirmed.

Missoula suffered a devastating loss. One Polson horse breeder lost seven horses in the fire; a Stevensville family lost six. We knew many of the people who lost horses. The rest of the fair that year felt gloomy, the smell of the charred barns heavy in the air. The fair, a cornerstone of rural community, created intimate bonds based more on participation than on mere entertainment. It pulled people together—in 1967 over heartbreaking loss—but usually over achievements. The community pledged its hearts and hands to the people who lost horses. 4-H taught me many things, but during true horror and adversity I also experienced the deep community connection that the fair fostered.

I PLEDGE MY HEAD TO CLEARER THINKING / 87

PHOTO 9. Hundreds of spectators watch a cattle show at the Missoula County Fair in the 1920s. The iconic Commercial Building with its two turrets, built in 1915, is visible in the background. Archives and Special Collections, Mansfield Library, University of Montana.

The fair was a way to keep Missoula's rural, ranching connections alive. That effect is much smaller now. The livestock are still shown and displayed at the fair, but the sheep and hog pens seem quite secondary to more urban displays of hot tubs and monster trucks. Exhibits of pies and tomatoes are insignificant. Missoula has become an urban center, not a community focused on supporting its agricultural region.

On Sunday, the last day of the 1967 fair, that feeling of teeming energy that started the fair has become a full, tired, satisfied feeling—overcast with sadness. While the fair is a celebration of individual and collective accomplishment, the fire has erased the festive atmosphere. The sheep barn, smelling of fresh straw on day one, smells of ripe manure on day five. Packing to leave is bittersweet; another 4-H year is complete and I have the guilty pleasure of knowing that, through pure luck, my horses are safe. I pack everything into my red tack box—ribbons, dirty clothes, and souvenirs from the carnival. School is in the air and the fairgrounds will soon go back to sleep. Riding home beside my mom in the red truck, I'm tired and saturated. I think I know what I have to do to seize the purple ribbon next year, but I've learned a deep lesson about how everything can go horribly wrong.

7

RAISED BY THE LAND

Life is like topography, Hobbes. There are summits of happiness and success, flat stretches of boring routine and valleys of frustration and failure.
        —Bill Watterson, *Calvin and Hobbes*, 1990

I understand the intimate contours of the Skyline Ranch from riding over it on Blue. She was a pedigreed Appaloosa, named Skyline Princess on her registration papers. Born in April 1964, she was half Arabian with a lovely dished face, fine bones, and the gray roan that so many Arabians display. Her main Appaloosa trait was a spotless white blanket that spread from her withers down over her rump, contrasting with a much darker gray tail. She stood only about fourteen hands high but commanded attention with her alert, intelligent presence.

We were a unit, a pair, for eighteen years. Most of our time together was solitary, and those were the hours that created the bond. Everyday life, particularly in summer, included casual rides up to the Big Pasture, often simply to ride and sometimes with work to do. Many people look back at precious times and places from childhood; mine are long rides on Blue, alone with my horse and my thoughts. The ranch was a quiet teacher and Blue my classmate.

I HAVE A BUCKET with enough oats to make that swishing, grainy sound that will lure Blue to me. I've walked out to the sheep pasture, where she's grazing halfway up the hill. After she ambles over, I let her munch a couple mouthfuls of grain—otherwise the bait won't work next time—and slip the halter over her head. After leading her down to the tack shack, where we store the horse gear, I tie her at the hitching post. Her eyes are half closed and sleepy in this warm part of the day, and her roached mane, grown out a couple of inches, gives her the look of a bored teenager with a mohawk.

I brush her down, running my hand over the raised V on the side of her neck. My parents burned the Skyline Ranch horse brand onto the right side of Blue's neck when she was a two-year old filly. When "calling" the brand, one would say it "Lazy V." The V falls down on its left side, so Blue had a "greater than" symbol stamped on her. Appropriate for an animal with great talent, drive, and devotion.

I put my thumb and forefinger into either side of her mouth so she'll open it for the bit. After buckling the chin strap, I throw my little knapsack over my back. I pull her up to a convenient overturned bucket so I don't have to jump so high to get on—cheating, since I'm a tall sixteen-year-old and have been riding bareback all my life. The bridle is the only gear we need this fine June morning. It's warm and sunny with a soft breeze. It takes us an hour to ride from the house to the farthest edge of the Big Pasture—a sequence of up, flat, down, up. That's up a half mile through the homeplace, flat a half mile along the 120/160 fence line, down through a big swale, then up again for a mile to the highest point in the North Hills—what we call The Top. Neighbors at the northeast corner of the Big Pasture called this morning to say that a couple of our cows are trespassing, so I'm supposed to bring them back and find out where they crawled through the fence.

We head up the dirt road away from the sprawling ranch buildings, past the big barn and the rows of haying equipment that will be in full swing next month. We climb along the two-track road that gains one thousand feet of elevation from the barnyard to The Top. As we get a quarter of a mile up, I breathe deeply and settle into the easy rhythm of Blue's gait. My mind opens up to daydream; I'm more comfortable up here in the hills than back at the buildings.

Blue and I are partners. We communicate through my shifting body weight and almost imperceptible movements of the reins. I trained Blue myself, spending hundreds of hours teaching her to lead, coaching her to accept a bit, and later a saddle. I learned to train horses from my dad, who did not "break" horses but gentled them. He taught me to be consistent; a few minutes of handling each day add up to a gentle, trusting animal. Blue was a fast learner—excitable but not flighty or silly. Once on her back, I taught her the subtle commands that I communicate through the bit and leg pressure. Even though she was usually compliant, we had our trials. Once, when I was training her to rein, she jerked sideways to a fence, putting a deep barbed-wire gash in the side of my knee. I learned that training horses in cutoffs is reckless; that's what chaps are for.

We walk right through the first gateway, because it's open to allow the sheep to use both pastures. We hug the fence between the Hundred and Twenty and the Hundred and Sixty. Mountain bluebirds flit along this half mile of barbed-wire fence, held up by old wooden posts put in by my grandfather. In my 4-H rangeland management project, I've learned that this grassland of rough fescue, Idaho fescue, rubber rabbit brush, western wheat grass, and needle grass is important for birds like the mountain bluebird and western meadowlark, which have adapted to use what native plants have to offer in the form of food, cover, and nesting. I love hearing the meadowlark, Montana's state bird, singing its ten beautiful up and down notes. Cavities in the posts are ideal nesting spots for bluebirds, which string out like sapphires on the fence. Daytime ground feeders, bluebirds are breathtaking cerulean flashes—hovering over the grasses to fly down and catch insects, or flying from a fence post to grab them.

As we move along the fence line, I think about last year's horse shows. I started a 4-H horse project in 1965, with Blue as a yearling, and then rode her at the fair for the next two years to display her skills. I have a color snapshot from last summer that shows me posed in the saddle in front of the barn, practicing for the fair. She was small and I was big. Where she was graceful and dainty for a horse, I was clumsy and big for a girl. I was only fifteen but had reached my adult height of five-foot-eight. The photo shows me in my shiny green pants over my boots in the stirrups, with a matching handmade western vest and my hair cropped at the chin. Blue had her back left hoof cocked up in a fidgety way. With my horse show get-up and Blue trimmed and brushed, we looked almost classy.

Today we're not out to prove ourselves. There are no ribbons at stake. I'm riding bareback in a T-shirt, cutoffs, and tennis shoes. My strong, tanned legs squeeze Blue's belly to balance my weight and control her gait. Nearing July, it's the end of the spring green-up season, and the grass is starting to turn a soft manila. On the flatter ground, cattle, sheep, and horses have gnawed it down by grazing across it this summer. I see a few head of cattle near a ridge line far above us, but it's the hottest part of the day and most of the cows are likely chewing their cud in the shady draws.

I climb back onto Blue after opening and closing the barbed-wire gate at the four corners, where N–S and E–W fence lines cross and the Big Pasture starts. It's a tough gate—I have to hug the post with both arms to squeeze the wire loop from the gate post. Repeat for closing it. My parents have grilled the ranching codes of conduct into me. Shut a gate if you find it that way.

Blue is eager to speed down through the big swale and then back up to the first water tank. I slow her to a walk by snugging the reins. Because she controls easily, I'm able to use a snaffle bit, which has a hinged piece of metal in her mouth. The snaffle does not magnify the pressure applied on the reins like a curb bit, with its solid bar across the tongue. She's not a "barn sour" horse—slow on the trip out from the barn but fast to return. We maintain a steady gait going up the hill, Blue's head lowered. I've learned to keep to the

PHOTO 10. Blue and the author in the Big Pasture at Skyline Ranch. The Missoula valley is shown in the background. Photo by Harriet Spurlock. Author's family collection.

high ground so we won't need to regain elevation we've already climbed. The beauty of experiencing the world on horseback is that I move fast enough to feel the lay of the land—the subtle shifts in elevation and aspect—but slow and close enough to see every detail of rock, weed, and badger hole. My years of caressing these hills on horseback have taught me how topography works.

We get to the first water trough in the Big Pasture. Blue buries her nose in the spring water. The tank is full, with slimy green algae at the edges. I hear a slow trickle as the small stream from the pipe makes water overflow on the downhill side, where a greener patch of grasses and low shrubs enjoy the excess moisture. We rest for a few minutes and then move back up the two-track, with large swatches of wildflowers on both sides. Some are just budding out and others are nearly done blooming. Together they paint the hillsides with half of the color wheel.

The second water trough is partway up Bear Draw, which runs northeast to southwest across the face of the Big Pasture and empties into a neighbor's land to the west. The draw, with its long swath of ponderosa pine, is visible from Missoula. We're at another hub, where we cross the draw to go up through a small valley we call the Basin. I've always loved this moist oasis—an edge where native shrubs bloom in the spring—chokecherry, serviceberry, rose, mock orange, and plum. It feels dark and mysterious in here. Only a tiny seep of water trickles out of the pipe above this tank, which connects to a natural spring. A sheen of dirty water lines the tank bottom. The ground around it is muddy, punctuated with overlapping hoofprints. The cattle have emptied this tank over the last day or two. My dad struggles to keep these troughs full, never fully knowing how the water moves underground and how to keep it flowing. At one point, he put a float on the tank so that water would stop trickling in when the tank was full and the surrounding ground would stay drier. But that forced the underground water to find another outlet, and the spring almost dried up. Today I'm only doing reconnaissance. My dad will return later and check that the pipes are gathering the spring water as he intends.

Blue and I climb up out of the lovely Basin on the western side. We will make the big circuit over the ridge line of the Big Pasture. That's not the shortest route to the fugitive cows, but I love this route. It will also take us the long way to the last water tank on the eastern side of the ranch. At The Top, Blue snorts and huffs after the long climb. This ridge is an ecological edge—the place where the dark forest falls northward for a half mile or so then rises toward the Rattlesnake Mountains. As we plod up the ridge, we can see to the north where a thicker, wetter forest stand includes Douglas fir and larch. This forest becomes impenetrable, darker and, to my teenage imagination, more foreboding. But the scattered, park-like ponderosas on the drier south-facing slope create a serene postcard in the foreground, widely scattered among grasses and wildflowers. The ranch buildings are not visible, but I have a 360-degree view of the Missoula valley. The long view south is out past the North Hills, over Missoula to the Bitterroot Mountains. To the east I can see the Clark Fork River as it curves around the base of Mount Jumbo, exiting Hellgate Canyon and entering the valley. We are at the same elevation as Mount Jumbo, which creates the eastern edge of the Rattlesnake Valley, also visible. Westward, I can scan the fertile fields of Grass Valley and the confluence of the Clark Fork and Bitterroot Rivers.

I slide down Blue's side and let her graze beside me as I sit on a log to eat my peanut butter and pickle sandwich—a favorite in my family. It is time for a little nap in the grass, and Blue can use a rest before the energy surge she'll need for chasing cattle. As I lie in the grass, I can see Blue's muzzle out at the end of the reins I'm holding. I know that I should not drop the reins because *no* horse is completely reliable, and I don't want to walk home. I ponder what the summer will bring for the two of us, not confident I can prepare her for the activities we have planned. At sixteen, I'm taking on more and more duties and challenges away from the serene times we spend on outings like this. Separate from 4-h, I will enter Blue in horse shows across western Montana. We compete in a range of classes that judge both her conformation and skill.

Like parents who drive their kids to hockey rinks or swimming pools at 5:00 a.m., my parents make sacrifices to pursue the horse show circuit in the summer. They transport not only me but Blue and other horses, saddles, hay, grain, and tools. And it often means mounting a camper on the back of the pickup so we have a place to sleep for a night or two. We are part of an amateur horse show culture, which is a big part of my parents' social life. For me, it's an education in responsibility and sportsmanship. This is a place where we are a team, where we connect over horsemanship. We choose the events we'll enter and celebrate together over winning a ribbon, even if it's not first place.

After a half hour of lounging, I move Blue downhill from me, jump up on her left side, hook my elbows over her backbone, and swing my right leg over. Now we head east across the ridge, where we can see the Rattlesnake Valley spread out below. At the ranch's eastern fence line, we turn north, checking for holes in the fence. After several minutes I see a place where the lowest wire of the fence is loose. It has red-brown cow hair clumped on the wire barbs. I make a mental note of this spot, prepared to tell my dad that the wire needs tightening—an easy fix as fencing chores go. Blue and I head for the gate into the neighbor's pasture, moving down through a pleasant meadow.

I don't find the cows right away because they are lying in a shady swale. We circle them. The two cows have brought their four-month-old calves along on their escapade. The calves jump up first, more flighty than their seasoned moms. Finally, the cows get to their feet when Blue and I are about fifty feet away. Blue is alert. She's watching them. We start moving the foursome toward the gate, the cows plodding and the animated calves darting one way, speeding ahead, charging off again. But they know to stay within some invisible radius of their moms. Blue and I ease them up the hill at a walk, and the cows seem resigned to going home as they amble toward the gate. As both cows and one calf go through, the other calf misses the gateway and swerves down the fence line. Its mother is trotting along our side of the fence. The calf is trying to join its mom by running next to her down the wrong side of the fence.

Blue darts to get around the calf. I'm holding tightly with both legs, one hand clutching the unclipped handle of mane at her withers. She loves this. Galloping downhill and out around the calf, she cuts it off at the fence and turns it back up the hill, away from its mother. Now it's bawling, confused, and panicked. It runs back toward the patch of matted grass where they bedded down. Blue anticipates the calf's every move, like a well-trained stock dog. She knows which way to dart exactly as I make the same decision; I don't need to use the reins. My shifting weight gives her direction. We get around the calf again, this time coaxing it back toward the gate opening. The baby runs through and sprints down the side of the fence to its mother and nuzzles up to her teat for security even as they're walking. Mom remains unconcerned as she ambles along the cow path.

I'm far more comfortable in a saddle when there's real work to do. It's easier to stay mounted; Blue loves cutting cattle so much that she'll veer out from under me in the heat of the chase. Earlier this month Blue and I, with several other mounted riders, rounded up the entire herd of one hundred cows and their calves for the annual branding session. I needed my cowboy boots set firmly in the stirrups for driving cattle in a serious way. We brand calves in early June after school is out. We can't do the job without a lot of help, so we invite friends and relatives for a work day that turns into a big party. I'm one of five or six wranglers who ride to the Big Pasture to find the cattle, bring them together, and herd them down to the corral. As they come over the hill from the Hundred and Sixty toward home, the cattle string out for a quarter of a mile, moving south. Riders try to keep them together as calves and the occasional cow break away in the wrong direction. It's loud and raucous. Cows bellow for their calves. Riders are whooping and hollering. The cattle funnel into the big corral beside the barn. Saddles can come off and the horses can rest. But the real work of the day gets underway with branding, vaccinating, castrating, and tagging the calves. Then it's time for beer and pop, potato salad, and grilled burgers.

I don't always bother with a saddle, and that casual attitude has gotten me into trouble. As in any close relationship, Blue and I sometimes let each other down. I have pushed her too hard on steep ground, chasing cattle or horses. When she let me down, I lay hurt on the ground. The worst episode was by the ranch dump, near a shallow draw at the edge of the ranch buildings. I trusted her too completely. Not only was I bareback but I rode with only a halter instead of a bridle. She took off running toward a barbed-wire fence. I was not in control. I panicked. She could run through or jump over that fence, leaving me bleeding, or worse, on the fence. In a split-second decision, I dove off onto my left side. She stopped abruptly at the fence. I'll never forget the walk back up to the house with a broken and dislocated shoulder. I lied and said that Blue had stumbled into a badger hole; I was too embarrassed to admit that I'd been riding her with only a halter. Careless rookie mistake, but I still felt betrayed by my horse.

Today in the summer heat, Blue can lollygag on our ride home. It's all downhill from here. We amble around the rough road that circles the eastern side of the Big Pasture, finding the third water trough in a narrow draw. In the early 1970s my parents hired neighbor Walt Carlson to dig a crude road around the 30-degree slope on the eastern side of the Big Pasture with his old D9 Caterpillar. The road gave access to a spring trickling from a small draw on this eastern side, but the scar of that road is still visible from the Rattlesnake Valley.

It is clear that the cattle haven't been over here in recent days and the tank is full. We continue downward toward home, opening and closing gates as we go. As the house and barnyard come into view at the gateway between the Hundred and Sixty and the homeplace, it's a short quarter of a mile down to the barn. First stop is the water tank at the edge of the corrals. This water comes from the same spring that supplies the house water. No one has ever drilled a well at Skyline Ranch. As the summer progresses in these dry hills, that spring will not supply all the water we need, and this tank will take priority. Washing clothes or irrigating the lawn can wait; the livestock must always have water.

We are back at the hitching post, and Blue has a dark, wet mark across her back and sides in the shape of my butt and legs. My thighs are dirty with horse hair, smelling of horse sweat. I brush her down with a curry comb and coo sweet words to her, telling her what a good girl she is. She lets me pick up her hooves to clean them, unconcerned, continuing to chew the last bits of grain in the bucket.

LIKE ME, BLUE LIVED an eclectic life—show horse, cow horse, even a few years as a racehorse. She spent most of her eighteen years at the ranch. Late in her life, she was with me and my new little family for a couple of years on a ranch near Bozeman, Montana. She died back at Skyline Ranch in 1982, lying on her side in the same small pasture, between the house and the barn, where I trained her as a filly and where she scraped my leg on the barbed wire. There was no veterinarian on hand since she went down fast. I was with her at the end. It felt like watching my childhood end and like the passing of a dear friend. I have a lovely braid from her mane and a much longer, grayer one from her tail. Her big heart, now still, had taken me through childhood from the age of twelve. Blue was a part of my life through the end of grade school, high school, college, and the early years of motherhood.

My rides on Blue were special partly because we were so close to town. From The Top I can see the city, where I also had a place. Growing up on the fringe means a foot in each of two worlds. This dichotomy shaped my childhood and young adulthood. Through Blue I learned about the land's form and function. I grew up with little supervision on the ranch but was schooled by every barbed-wire fence, pine tree, and rocky outcrop. I was partly raised by this landscape, by those rounded hills and the hard lessons they held. And I came to understand not only the land's topography but the contours of my own family and ranching culture. Blue was a big part of that education. Animals bond to place. Caring for them and working with them bonds *us* to place.

On the one hand, the land is part of me; I am rooted in the North Hills. On the other, I've lived most of my adulthood in the other world and funneled my interest in rural, changing landscapes into a profession. I take comfort in the fact that, all these years later, my grandchildren can have the same type of experiences at Skyline Ranch. The weeds are spreading, but the land is resilient and unpaved. The bluebirds were scarce for decades but are now coming back. Water still trickles from the ranch's precious springs. Those grandkids can ride to The Top and look out over Missoula from the same perch, dreaming their own stories.

8

ALL LIVESTOCK SOLD AS IS

The farmer is the only man in our economy who buys everything at retail, sells everything at wholesale, and pays the freight both ways.
—John F. Kennedy, 1960

The Hereford cow lurches down the chute as my dad swats her rump to keep her moving out of the horse trailer. The veterinarian pregnancy-tested our cows last week, and this one came up dry. She didn't "take" during the May weeks that the bull was out to pasture with the cows. There's no use feeding her for another year, particularly since she is eight years old, past middle age for a stock cow. We're backed up to the chutes at the east end of the yards. The chutes consist of two parallel wooden ramps with plank sides six feet tall, to allow farmers to offload livestock from their vehicles. Truck exhaust fumes mix with the ever-present odors of manure, cigarettes, and chewing tobacco. Farmers and ranchers unload livestock early in the morning. Dad will drop me off at high school after this errand, and I'll be back to the yards after school.

"Hey Jim! Warm morning for October, huh? Just bringing in a dry cow," my dad shouts to the guy tracking incoming livestock from a small plywood hut next to the chutes.

"Yeah, give me a minute to get these damn steers out of the way," says Jim. They gab about the weather as our cow paces in the small pen at the bottom of the chute, and several steers amble down the chute next to ours. I have no attachment to this cow, so selling her doesn't bother me. I stay in the cab to listen to the Beatles, quickly changing the dial from Dad's country station. Jim scrawls on the intake paperwork and then slaps a yellow sticker with a black "249" on the cow's rump. The number matches the receipt with my dad's name. We pull away from the chute to let an old, muddy Ford pickup back in with three Hereford yearlings inside a wooden stock rack. There's now a line of six vehicles waiting to unload trailers and trucks of all sizes, and our cow begins her all-day voyage from the east to the west end of the Missoula Livestock Auction.

I can see not only the upper reaches of Skyline Ranch from the yards but the ranch house tucked in its fold of land. The ranch sits only about a mile and a half away as the crow flies. My parents and grandparents had long bought and sold livestock at the yards, and proximity is a clear benefit. When Grandpa was alive, he could sit in the bleachers to check the value of steers in the morning and, if prices were up, go home and load a few head to sell in the afternoon. Few farmers had that luxury.

Missoula's stockyards opened in the late 1930s when Bill Schaan leased a one-fourth-mile-long strip of property from Northern Pacific Railroad. The land paralleled the tracks west of downtown and the West Side neighborhood. After Schaan built the auction barn and corral complex, cattle buyers could ship animals out on trains. Well into the 1960s, cattle moved by rail, destined for midwestern feedlots. Later, rail traffic stopped due to the decentralization of meat packing, increased truck haulage, and the completion of the interstate highway system. Now, eighteen-wheelers with "bullrack" trailers haul cattle and other livestock. Over 65,000 head of cattle passed through the yards each year in the 1960s and 1970s—the heydays of cattle commerce in Missoula. Ranchers from as far north as the Canadian border and as far south as southern Idaho brought cattle to sell. In contrast, the auction yard sold only around 20,000 head in the 2010s.

In addition to cattle going out of Missoula by rail, others came in that way. Livestock cars packed with dirty, stinking cattle rumbled through Missoula in those days, moving steers from Washington to Nebraska and Kansas feed lots. They stopped in Missoula for just a few hours. Policies prevented the railroad from leaving livestock on train cars for extended periods. The shipper was obliged to honor a Feed, Water, Rest (FWR) provision that varied from twenty-four to thirty-six hours. Coming from the West Coast, trains unloaded cattle into the pens at the Missoula yards for FWR. Once my parents were playing canasta at the ranch with Sid, the yards foreman, and his wife. Around midnight Sid got a call that a cattle train had come in and the cattle needed to be unloaded, fed, and watered. So the two couples drove to the yards and took care of the cattle. The interruption was as routine as the card game itself, just part of what people did living on a ranch close to the stockyards.

Now as my dad and I drive off, another yards employee lets our cow out of the pen. She ambles into a broad fenced alley flanked on both sides by a warren of smaller alleys and straw-lined wooden pens. Some are big enough to hold six head, while others can accommodate thirty. He opens the gate to a small pen and she trots in, surrounded by a cacophony of bellowing cows and calves. She'll wait all morning until her appearance in the sale ring and her departure by truck, several hours later, through chutes at the west end of the yards.

LIKE THE SALES RING, my parents' Stockyard Cafe hummed with activity—not with an auctioneer's chant, but the clink of thick coffee mugs, spoons clanking against stainless steel, sizzling bacon on the grill, and continual chatter and laughter. On very busy sale days, from 1964 to 1972, a half dozen of us worked there, including me and my parents, my grandmother, aunt, cousins, and various other relatives.

The shed-roofed café was a small addition to a large cinder-block building, the Top Cut sales barn, which sat across a big gravel parking lot from the Missoula Livestock Auction sales barn. The café had no sign; everyone just knew it as the Stockyard Cafe and expected it to be open only on sale days. The café enjoyed strong western light coming through mullioned windows.

The rhythm of the entire stockyards, or "yards" as the locals called it, affected the café. Diesel eighteen-wheelers idled. Cows bawled for their calves. Ranchers hollered greetings across the parking lot. Except on cold winter days, the café door stood open and a battered screen door kept out flies. Even before stepping inside, one could smell apple pies baking, or catch the aroma of a big roast in the oven, destined for hot beef sandwiches—thick slices spread over white bread, topped with gravy. Mashed potatoes on the side.

The café's main room housed the kitchen, surrounded by an L-shaped counter with twenty round, spinning stools. A separate dining room held six green Naugahyde-covered booths. Brand inspectors, ranchers, and cattle buyers sat on the backless stools, drinking coffee and eating ham and eggs. For entertainment they watched my dad roll out pie crusts on a big floury maple board for a dozen or more pies. Bill Randolph came in every week for a piece of lemon meringue. The semi-truck drivers—some from as far away as Spokane or Billings—drank gallons of coffee (ten cents a cup; free refills) while waiting for their cargo. One of them kept his medicine in our refrigerator.

OUR WORK REVOLVED AROUND the weekly cattle sales. Mom recently explained that Thursdays were big days even when she and my dad ran their first business, the Trail Cafe, from 1957 to 1962. That restaurant was a couple of miles closer to town. Mom said, "It's when you'd see a lot of ranching people you knew. They'd come into the Trail and all the restaurants on the west end of town." When farmers brought their weaned steers to occasional Monday "feeder" sales, they'd treat themselves to a restaurant lunch. Sometimes the yards held a special Saturday sheep sale. The Horse and Dairy Cow sales on the first Tuesday of each month brought in yet another clientele. The June horse sale was the biggest of the year, a "big pay day" for the café, according

PHOTO 11. Harriet and Bud Spurlock at their Trail Cafe on West Broadway, Missoula, in the 1950s. Unknown photographer. Author's family collection.

to my mom. "Everybody came to the June horse sale, and everybody ate at the café."

The hour right after lunch is the sweet spot for the best livestock prices. Cattle generally go through the sales ring in the order they are brought in, at least within a certain category—canner cows, feeder calves, bulls. But it's not quite that simple. My parents would often slip a fifth of Jack Daniels to Sid, who had considerable control over the order of sales.

At 1:30 p.m. a wrangler named Steve opens the gate letting our cow into the alley toward the sales ring. In the 1960s and 1970s, some young guys with rural roots left high school and worked odd jobs, including sale days at the yards. Many ended up in Vietnam and some never came back. Steve swings a long whip to keep cattle moving. He flashes it in the air, making a distinctive crack. The whip meets hide with a duller snap. Growing up, I didn't think twice about the way we treated the animals with whips, branding irons, and dehorners. I now cringe with far more empathy.

ALL LIVESTOCK SOLD AS IS / 105

Our cow trots toward the real action at the indoor sale barn, which is full of people by midmorning. Spectators climb a two-story outside stairway to a broad deck facing east. They can scan over hundreds of milling, noisy, muddy cattle in a checkerboard of pens. Since last night was cold, steam rises from manure piles and the air is ripe. Looking down, one can see the maze of catwalks above all the alley and pen fences. The catwalks are two-by-twelve-inch planks, with strategically placed stairs, on which employees walk to move around the yards without bothering with gates. This is a secondary circulation system above the cattle. Walking the catwalks requires good balance and orientation; occasional falls end in broken bones.

People enter the auction building from the deck and arrive at the top of steep indoor bleachers. The heart of the yards is a small sales ring where two or three hands with shitty boots and whips keep the cattle moving so buyers can see them from all sides. The crowd of a couple hundred people includes ranchers selling stock or buying a few head, professional buyers for the big feedlots, and people sizing up what steers are bringing per pound. A sign warns: *This Is A Cash Market—All Livestock Sold As Is.* Other boards ring the wall high above the auctioneer, advertising local businesses—banks, feed stores, ranch supply outlets. Howard Raser, the auctioneer and yards owner, settles into his seat in an elevated booth on the opposite side of the ring from spectators. "Let's sell a few cows!" Next to him, a recorder documents sale prices and tracks the numbers on those rump stickers. In each corner, a four-foot-tall metal shield is bolted to the floor, safe havens for the handlers when a big cow puts her head down and charges.

Before I was ten, I had learned to interpret Howard's amplified staccato. He cajoles to get a higher bid, his hand waves across the crowd to keep track of multiple bidders, and he jokes with a guy in the ring as a rangy bull threatens to charge.

Howard knew everybody. He and the other auctioneers he hired were some of the most well-known and respected members of the rural community. Some institutions become so closely associated with their owners that the two are nearly inseparable. Howard was the face of Missoula Livestock Auction. He was from the Platte River country of Nebraska and, indeed,

106 / STORIES FROM THE EDGE

seemed more of a midwestern gentleman than a Montana cowboy, wearing nice Pendleton wool jackets and a wool fedora instead of a cowboy hat. He once corrected my mom, telling her that chickens are not butchered, they are "dressed." In the 1950s the federal government convicted Howard of a tax crime and sent him to prison in Washington. He was so well-loved and needed by ranching families that hundreds of people signed petitions to keep him free. Of course that didn't sway the IRS, and he spent some time behind bars. After that, he continued as a solid statesman of Missoula County's rural community. He even served as a parole officer for another released prisoner he had served with—a first in Montana criminal justice.

Howard generally knows who is buying. His weekly calls to Omaha help him know the prices he should seek. Kids and newcomers learn early not to talk with their hands but to sit on them. An auctioneer might interpret somebody's wild swat at flies as a raised bid. A sign tells casual observers: *The First Two Rows Reserved for Buyers Only.* The buyers sit in theater seats down front, their boots up on taut steel cables that separate them from the livestock. They work on commission for Armour, Swift, and other big packing companies, bidding against a couple of local packing outfits. They look for specific animals—maybe twenty head of pregnant Angus heifers or 500–700-pound weaned calves. Like the yards itself, buyers are middlemen in the livestock system. A small phone booth sits in a corner near the "good seats" so buyers can communicate with their clients. It's a Missoula version of the New York Stock Exchange, with brokers taking orders, relaying prices, and tracking financial trends.

Swinging gates choreograph a stream of livestock flowing through the sales ring. A wiry old cowboy swings the "in-gate" open, and our #249 sprints into the sales ring looking panicked and agitated. She sports a shaved area on her right hip where a brand inspector has revealed one of Skyline Ranch's three registered brands, the Lazy K Hanging Eight. Brand inspectors from the Montana Department of Livestock work out of each of Montana's thirteen stockyards. They inspect each animal before it sells, making sure that the seller is the legal owner, as proven by state-registered brands.

"Sold at eighteen cents a pound." Our cow has been in the ring less than a minute, and she'll most likely become dog food. After Howard gets his final bid, one of the cowboys in the ring opens the "scale gate," letting the cow—no longer ours—out of the ring and onto the scales. She sprints out, eager to leave the limelight. After she's weighed, Bill Randolph pulls the "out-gate" open with a rope, and the cow enters the long alley toward pens on the west end. In -20° winters and 100° summers, Thursday after Thursday for twenty-five years, Bill stood outdoors, pulling that same gate open and closed. Later in the afternoon our cow will join dozens of other "canners" on a semi heading out of Missoula.

That evening, ranchers will bemoan how little they got for their cattle. I found a yellowed, undated *Minnesota Times* clipping in Grandma Kramen's 1944 diary, written by an "Ivanhoe." I'm sure she loved the satire.

> Livestock are animals that are bred and raised in the country to keep farmers broke and the buyer crazy. They are born in the spring, mortgaged in the summer, pasteurized in the fall, and given away in winter. They vary in size, color, weight and the man who guesses their nearest weight and market grade is called a "livestock buyer" by the public, a robber by the farmer, a poor risk by the banker, and a "bologna peddler" by Mrs. O'Brien. The price of livestock is usually set at the Chicago stockyards and invariably goes up after you have sold and down when you hold. When you have light ones, they want heavy and when you have cattle you find they want sheep or vice versa. If you have steers they want bulls, if you have cows they want heifers. If you have calves they say they are running a special on veal. When they are thin the top price is for the fat and when they are fat you are told the tallow market is now shot to hell. Twenty years ago I swore I'd quit the business then and there but here we are with a ton of critters depending on us to sell them to someone.

The Stockyard Cafe was the second café my parents ran when I was a kid. From the ages of five through ten I spent large swaths of time in the kitchen of my parents' first business, the Trail Cafe. It faced Highway 10, or Broadway Street, the main east–west road through Missoula before the freeway existed. My school was in the West Side neighborhood, on the opposite side of Broadway from the café, and my mother would not let me cross the street alone. I'd walk from the school and she'd watch for me as she waited tables. After a bit of a wait I would see her coming across to collect me, wearing her waitress uniform, starched cap, and apron. Starting when I was six or seven, I would peel a hundred-pound burlap bag of potatoes after school each day. Then I'd feed the peeled spuds through a hand-operated French-fry cutter mounted on the wall. The regulars teased me about often falling asleep on top of a bag of spuds. They called me Sputnik, for the Soviet satellite launched on my fifth birthday.

Later, the Stockyard Cafe was a regular part of my life from the age of eleven to eighteen. My brother Ken was there from infancy to his early years of elementary school. As a first and second grader, groggy Ken would drag along to the café at 6:00 a.m., where he'd have breakfast. Then after the Eddy's Bread delivery guy dropped off our trays of hamburger buns and white sandwich bread, he'd take Ken to school, his next delivery stop.

The Stockyard Cafe supplemented my parents' ranch income. Like many ranchers, they needed a second income since the ranch could not fully support a family. For Bill Randolph it was swinging the "out gate." For my parents it was slinging hash browns and baking pies. Just as the ranch was both a working ranch and a part of extended Missoula, my parents were both ranchers and townspeople. We relied on relatives to help brand cattle, but also to wait tables. My maternal grandmother, Mildred, was a dependable helpmate. She pitched in wherever needed—washing dishes, making sandwiches, or pouring refills. I still don't understand why customers called her Grandma rather than Mildred, since in the 1960s she was only in her fifties! Some of those guys sitting on the stools were older than she. Grandma taught me to play cribbage sitting in a booth in the back room during lulls in afternoon business.

Even though the café was open only on Thursday, the sale meant a three-day job for us. Wednesday was cleaning, buying food, and cooking. Then the sale day itself, and Friday for cleaning up and dealing with leftover food. When sales ran far into the evening, the stockyard owners would determine if they might adjourn until Friday or stay late. If they decided to finish up on

Thursday night, someone from the yard's office would ask us to deliver a hundred sandwiches to the sales ring. I'd lay long rows of Wonder bread out on the counter and create an assembly line of sliced ham, iceberg lettuce, American cheese, and mayonnaise. During the week between sales, we stocked up on nonperishable goods from local wholesalers, including cigarettes and chew. Delivery trucks brought perishable food early on sale days—meats, bread, and milk.

The Top Cut Hereford Show and Sale in early spring provided the cultural and economic highlight of each year. The big reddish-brown bulls, with their white faces, lounged in the concrete block pavilion attached to the café. Proximity to the sale put us in the midst of excitement and glamour. The smell of hot coffee blended with the aroma of shampoos for grooming the bulls, sawdust and shavings for bull bedding, and of course manure. I spruced up my steers for the fair every August, but here I was among the professionals. The bull breeders polished, groomed, and protected the bulls like prized racehorses. The Top Cut, one of Missoula's oldest ranch traditions, started in the 1940s and ran until 1999. Cattle companies from across the West brought purebred Hereford bulls to show and sell. This was before marketers created a buzz around Angus beef in the minds of consumers.

Crowds of five hundred or more people were on hand to see grand champion bulls sell for upward of $10,000. In the twenty-first century, they can sell for hundreds of thousands. A 1967 advertisement in a Washington newspaper claimed that "This is the largest Hereford event between Denver and Calgary. Where else but in Missoula can you find 500 to select from?" Although I was wearing cutoffs as I poured coffee for these ranchers, I felt like I was attending the Oscars.

When other baby boomer kids were—what *were* they doing?—I was spending my extracurricular time at the café. The yards was more a social hub for me than high school. My first boyfriend was Howard Raser's nephew, and later I dated a young brand inspector. Even though I waited tables, washed dishes, and helped cook on sale days, the times I most remember are the days when I was there alone. Always an introvert, I never minded being at the café by myself on Wednesdays after school. My parents sent me to make a couple of gallons of pie filling for the banana cream, coconut cream, and chocolate cream pies. I stirred the scalding milk in big stainless steel double boilers, snitching a Baby Ruth from the candy rack. I often rode my moped to get there, and later my first car, a little blue Fiat. On Fridays, I'd mop the floors, wash pots and pans, and put leftover food away. My family always ate well, since leftovers from sale days sustained us for the rest of the week.

I went on to reenact my parents' dual roles. As young adults with a baby son, my husband and I leased a ranch in Missoula's Grass Valley west of town. We milked cows, put up hay, and dabbled in the beef cattle business. Our side hustle was a familiar enterprise. In 1976 we started the Old Town Cafe, a popular breakfast place on Missoula's Skid Row. I used the skills I'd grown up with, and some of the same equipment from the Stockyard Cafe. I rolled out crusts for a dozen pies a day and made cream pie filling using the same recipe my dad used, starting with two gallons of scalding milk. We catered to a more urban clientele that lined up down the block on Saturday mornings for huevos caliente. The demand for hot beef sandwiches on white bread had dried up.

Books chronicling Missoula's history discuss the founders—bankers and businessmen who created downtown and historic neighborhoods. But written histories make no mention of the livestock auction, even though it was a critical anchor for agriculture. Ranching was once one of the valley's main industries. Authors have documented the sugar beet plant, ice house, brewery, and many other businesses, both prominent and obscure. They have neglected Missoula's smelly, noisy livestock sales ring.

The original sales ring burned in the 1980s. After a short stint of selling livestock outdoors, new owners moved the auction about ten miles west of town. Now people buy and sell livestock and horses online, and ranchers see each other at the grain elevator, schools, and funerals. The only evidence of the stockyard site's fifty-year heritage is now a few road names. Stockyard Road, a short connector street behind the old stockyards site, is an incongruous address for the Hilton, which looms at six stories at one end. Howard Raser Drive runs parallel to Stockyard Road near the freeway. Those are hollow designations.

ALL LIVESTOCK SOLD AS IS / 111

The yards served a purpose well beyond agricultural enterprise. Like the county fair, the yards functioned as a hub for rural social life in the valleys radiating from Missoula. It served as a weekly gathering place. It might have been the only place you ever ran into your neighbor—giving you both a chance to complain about the weather and speculate about the price of hay. People sat on the hard bleacher seats to discuss cattle prices and the other trials of irrigating, calving, fencing, and haying. Just as importantly, they gossiped about weddings, babies, land sales, and other human goings-on in rural communities. They continued those conversations over a burger and milkshake at the Stockyard Cafe. My family had a specific role in that rural community.

The railroad company, now Montana Rail Link, tore down the auction barn and the maze of wooden corrals, returning the land to its railroad roots. Piles of railroad ties and assorted equipment scatter across that acreage now. The area feels abandoned and empty, another industrial LULU on the wrong side of the tracks. The only remaining structure is the cinder-block Top Cut Sale barn with its modest lean-to addition, where my family's café once hummed. I feel melancholy when I drive past, remembering the community bonds, agricultural commerce, and meals built at the yards.

9

WATER RUNS DOWNHILL

We abuse land because we regard it as a commodity belonging to us. When we see land as a community to which we belong, we may begin to use it with love and respect.

—Aldo Leopold, *A Sand County Almanac*, 1949

After my timid knock, I'm invited into Professor Tom Birch's office at the University of Montana in September 1971. As a sophomore not yet nineteen, I'm here to talk my way into a senior-level course called Wilderness Philosophy. Professor Birch holds weekly seminars throughout the twelve-week quarter, but students chew the real philosophical meat on mandatory weekend backpacking trips into western Montana's backcountry. The syllabus shows sessions in the Selway-Bitterroot Range and the Mission Mountains. The former became a federally designated wilderness only seven years before. The latter was then on the brink of wilderness designation.

The course was part of UM's new Round River program, named for Aldo Leopold's essay claiming that ecological study enriches a person's land ethic and strengthens community. Round River led to the Wilderness Institute at the university, started in 1975, which still emphasizes immersion in field courses.

As I stand fidgeting in his tiny office, Professor Birch leans back and waves toward a chair. "Why do you want to take a senior-level course on wilderness? And how fit are you for hiking in the mountains?" I explain that I enjoyed an introductory philosophy course and made good grades as a freshman. Then I offer my real claim: "I grew up on a local ranch and I've been doing hard work outside my whole life." With a small grin, he signs my petition. I reflect on my answer fifty years later with a mix of amusement and embarrassment. I soon learned that carrying a fifty-pound backpack uphill on the Kraft Creek trail in the Missions is a far different thing than chasing cattle by horseback all day or waiting tables for ten hours. I wasn't as tough as I thought.

At nineteen I believed that knowing working lands gave me, if not a head start, at least a different perspective on nature. A billion acres, about half the land in the entire lower forty-eight states, are working lands that provide food, timber, and other resources for peoples' benefit. Imagine a transect that runs from the heart of the city, out to the small towns and suburbs, further to the farm fields, on to wide-open grazing and ranching lands, beyond to the logged timber tracts, and finally into the deepest wilderness. I spent my early years halfway along that gradient. I felt that I came from the doorstep of wilderness. Geographically, I did. The 33,000-acre Rattlesnake Wilderness, designated by Congress in 1980, is a little over three miles from the northern edge of Skyline Ranch. Though naive, I would not claim that the ranch was untamed, but I had the sense that I knew the lay of the land—at least one piece of it, and that this knowledge gave me an affinity for more pristine places.

I thought that a ranch upbringing was a good prerequisite for knowing the wilds of western Montana and for penetrating the ideas of Henry David Thoreau, Aldo Leopold, and Edward Abbey. I didn't know much about lands wilder than Skyline Ranch. I had been in the true wilderness only a couple of times. My family took pack trips into high mountain lakes, deep into what is

114 / STORIES FROM THE EDGE

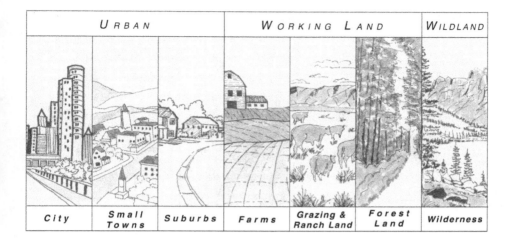

now the Rattlesnake Wilderness. Wilderness Philosophy helped me explore ideas about the relationship of rural to wild land. Henry David Thoreau wrote, "I see young men, my townsmen, whose misfortune it is to have inherited farms, houses, barns, cattle, and farming tools; for these are more easily acquired than got rid of... Who made them serfs of the soil?"

Aldo Leopold developed his land ethic almost a century later. Compared with Thoreau, he was far more optimistic about the farmer's relationship to nature. "What more delightful avocation than to take a piece of land and by cautious experimentation to prove how it works. What more substantial service to conservation than to practice it on one's own land?" It is interesting that Thoreau, Leopold, and Abbey were born and raised in small eastern and midwestern towns, then veered to the pastoral and wild side of the transect in their writing and their life paths.

Edward Abbey: "May your trails be crooked, winding, lonesome, dangerous, leading to the most amazing view. May your mountains rise into and above the clouds. It is not enough to fight for the land; it is even more important to enjoy it. While you can."

I wasn't aware of the growing conflicts between ranchers and environmentalists. Birch's wry smile should have given me a clue. The west was becoming a battleground between the wild and the pastoral. This war is not over. As I write this, many decades later, the wolves-versus-ranchers debate is feverish. A *Missoulian* headline reads: "Wolves Kill 120 Sheep." Public meetings elicit "check-your-guns-at-the-door" mandates. While landowners and conservation groups have protected hundreds of thousands of acres of privately owned farmland from development over the past forty years, the controversy remains about how working lands relate to wildness. Flash points in the west are grazing rights and extractive uses on public lands. We expect those lands to provide not only grazing for livestock but habitat for many wildlife species, timber, minerals, and recreation, among other resources. That's a tall order, rife with controversy and incompatibility.

Wilderness Philosophy changed my life. Professor Birch was young, handsome, and charismatic, only two years beyond his PhD. He knew his way around the back country. On a Friday before a weekend outing, Birch invited the eight seminar students to his house in the Rattlesnake neighborhood to pack gear. He joked that he had so many lightweight gadgets he could barely carry his pack. Over backcountry campfires, we discussed the seminal works in wilderness thinking, debating issues around land use, wildlife, and motorized access. Most students were men from various Montana towns or other states. There was not another ranch kid in the class. I was painfully aware of a town-gown divide, and it felt even wider for me because I came from a working-class ranching family. I've straddled that divide ever since. At backcountry campsites, my introverted nature was challenged by the intimate proximity of older students I barely knew. It was also soothed by wilderness as a state of mind, by the fear and wonder that come from being alone in nature.

I was shy—soaking up ideas but feeling that I didn't have much to offer. Although I didn't realize it then, I was beginning a lifelong curiosity about land and its uses. I was forming my adult worldview: that humans should leave some wild lands untouched and that ecological integrity is vital for the lands we do use. I started to see the North Hills as a pivot point—a place bridging city and wildness on that urban-to-wild transect.

The protection of wilderness is so controversial that fifty years after passage of the Wilderness Act, we have designated only 3.5 million acres in

Montana (3.75 percent of the fourth largest state). Until the 2013 addition of 67,000 acres to the Bob Marshall Wilderness on the Rocky Mountain Front, Congress had created the last wilderness area in 1983. Missoula is a microcosm of those issues, a city where only a small band of farm and ranch land separates it from the wilderness. Environmentalists rubbed shoulders with loggers and ranchers in watering holes downtown when Missoula was still a working-person town. Far less so now.

Wilderness Philosophy did not pitch me into a life of wilderness study, and I've been only a quiet advocate. Yet, it sparked my curiosity about how people relate to the lands along the middle of the city-to-wilderness transect. My personal and professional life gave me plenty of perspective about the urban end and the rural middle. Fifty years later, I'm far more at ease in the city than in the wilderness, and I'm still drawn to the places between them.

John, a twenty-year-old student from Livingston, Montana, was the son of a railroad conductor and a nurse. He lived in the rental log cabin at Skyline Ranch. We both enrolled in the course because we were spending a lot of time together. Among other attractions, we shared back-to-the-land ideals. John and I married in 1972 and in 1975, four years after Wilderness Philosophy, we were young landless ranchers with a baby. We were trying to find our own place, geographically, personally, and professionally. We leased fertile farmland in Grass Valley west of Missoula, knowing we would likely never be able to buy a place of our own. We lived in a turn-of-the-century two-story brick farmhouse that stood on a bench facing Mullan Road, the first wagon road to cross the Rocky Mountains toward the West Coast in the mid-nineteenth century. Before that it was Saleesh Road, an ancient Indian trail. The barn, corrals, and farmland spread out below the bench in the wide floodplain of the Clark Fork River. I milked a Jersey cow and sold raw milk to townspeople. We owned a small herd of Hereford cows and grew lush alfalfa hay for winter feed. Like many farmers, we were tethered to summer irrigation—changing sprinkler pipes twice a day and coaxing water along small ditches in flood-irrigated fields, where gravity and removable tarp dams guided water to saturate plant roots.

One morning I stood behind the house on the edge of the bench, side by side with Bill, the ranch's owner. Bill was of my parents' generation; he knew John and me well and mentored us in ranching. As we looked south over the fields, I mentioned that John would be away for a few days. "I can handle the irrigation while he's gone," I said.

"No, you need to know the lay of the land to irrigate."

He believed that I lacked the innate feel for how water flowed, where the land was higher and lower. He felt that my young husband had those skills, even though John was green in ranching. Over the past couple of years my dad had taught him everything he knew about cattle, haying, machinery . . . and irrigating. I milked cows, baled hay, pulled calves, and worked hard alongside John in the entire ranching enterprise. I had grown up on the family ranch, working outside year around—chasing cattle, bucking bales, training horses, mending fences. My brother, and only sibling, was eleven years younger so I hauled tools in my dad's footsteps as his "right hand man" for my entire childhood and adolescence.

I wasn't assigned the irrigation job. I remember thinking, "How is it that John knows the lay of the land and I don't?" Because he was a man. This was paradoxical because my parents never cast me in a frilly feminine role. They expected hard physical labor from me. But decisions about the land, even about manipulating the way water flowed, were for men.

People have often ignored or dismissed women's love and knowledge of the land. None of the writers we studied in Wilderness Philosophy were women; a similar course now would likely include the voices of Terry Tempest Williams, Annie Dillard, and Gretel Ehrlich. Ranching women in the 1970s were still called ranch-wives. But in the twenty-first century, one hears them called ranchers. The number of farms owned and operated by women is increasing in recent decades, with nearly a quarter million female farm and ranch owners in the U.S. Many have inherited their land or were widowed, but increasing numbers of younger women are choosing farming careers. In 2019 the *New York Times* ran a story on this topic. They documented that long before white settlement, Indigenous women "tended and tamed vast fields, traversed rugged landscapes with their dogs, hunted, raised livestock."

In 2012, 14 percent of the 2.1 million farms and ranches in the United States were run by women, according to the USDA. The agency expects that ratio to rise because over half of the farms and ranches are expected to change hands within twenty years. This is a cultural shift. The *Times* quotes a woman rancher, Ms. Carmen, in Oregon: "The number of times I've walked into a meeting and people are like, 'you don't look like a rancher.' . . . But the same judgment proved liberating, as female ranchers like Ms. Carmen redefined the job. 'If I don't look like a rancher,' she said, 'I don't have to act like one all of the time, right?'"

Women have written eloquent stories about their roles outside the farm kitchen and garden and their connections to the larger landscape. Willa Cather pioneered a path for women's voices in rural places, weaving beautiful, though fictional, human stories with the lands they inhabited. She advised authors: "Let your fiction grow out of the land beneath your feet." Over the past twenty-five years, other female authors have explored their ranch roles in stories about leaving the land. Like me, Judy Blunt left the ranch. In *Breaking Clean* she explored the first three decades of her life on lonesome eastern Montana ranches and her flight from that life. Mary Clearman Blew grew up on a small cattle ranch in Montana and chronicled that life and her escape from it in *All but the Waltz: Essays on a Montana Family*. These women, and others, continue to describe the way women know and love their land and their situations relative to it. Our attachment is compromised by the fact that we leave the land for other pursuits—marriage, offspring, education, a job in town, a career.

Like these other writers, my path took me to academia and a life far from the ranch. Staying was not an option in my life circumstances. After a few years of ranching on leased land, owning and operating a restaurant, and supporting John's college education, I enrolled at Washington State University once our two boys were in elementary school. My three years at the University of Montana a decade earlier had earned me a minor in anthropology and enough transfer credits to give me a head start toward a degree, even though I was changing majors. Landscape Architecture combined my interests in art and natural resources. I learned subdivision design, plant identification, and site engineering. The latter holds one primary truth—that water runs downhill. But I already knew that from riding Blue and traversing the Big Pasture's draws and hillsides. The bachelor's program in landscape architecture required me to take a course in irrigation design, although it focused on gardens and lawns, not hay. Instead of mucking around in the mud for flood irrigation, its only focus was laying out sprinkler systems. Studio design courses were an outlet for my artistic tendencies, even though garden design was not my professional interest. Instead, I wanted to consider large landscapes like the view from The Top of the Big Pasture looking south over Missoula. I sought to understand and affect the way rural and urban land butt against one another, trying to apply landscape architecture principles to rural places. I had a mentor who helped me deepen those interests and paved a way for me to continue. I studied landscape planning in one of the most densely developed and micro-planned countries on earth—the Netherlands. A master's degree in landscape planning from a Dutch university helped launch my career.

I practiced as a working landscape architect for only a short period; I wanted to conduct research and write, and an academic path satisfied my introverted nature. By this point I had overcome shyness and gained a voice, finding that my ranch background provided unique perspectives within the profession. I was undaunted by the scarcity of women in academia, although gender issues proved challenging. I was only the third woman to be hired in the University of Michigan's School of Natural Resources (now School for Environment and Sustainability), a unit that had started as a Forestry Department in 1903. In my first few years there, faculty men were still holding evening poker parties to which women were not invited.

My research asked where to expand urban areas while protecting vulnerable agricultural land, examining the forces that shape rural places at the margins of towns and cities. During my sixteen years teaching, I developed a seminar class for graduate students titled "Landscape Planning in Rural Environments," which explored the issues that affect change in rural landscapes. I introduced students to the natural, historical, agricultural, social, and scenic factors that affect physical patterns on farmland and small rural communities.

We examined farmland protection, historic landscape preservation, sustainable agriculture, and farm policy. I was careful to include women's voices in reading assignments. Unlike the Wilderness Philosophy model, we took no hikes in the backcountry (or, more appropriately, on Michigan farms), but I hoped to spur new ideas about preserving rural places among these bright graduate students seeking advanced degrees in natural resources and urban planning.

I was learning as well. I remained curious about patterns—starting from those I could see from The Top of the Big Pasture and then expanding to metropolitan areas around North America. The ideas from Wilderness Philosophy stuck throughout my career, and it was compelling to apply them to working lands. I've been studying the lay of the land my entire life, through travel, in academic research, and within the lines of my writing. I've learned from many women who kept working lands in their hearts. After leaving academia in 2005, I continued to focus on the conservation of rural places in my consulting business—my fourth career after rancher, restaurateur, and professor. By then, I had started to be alarmed about the housing developments inching toward Skyline Ranch. When I returned to Missoula, consulting with land trusts across the west was a surrogate for conserving the ranch. I'm still working toward that goal.

10

BOXCAR BLUES

I let it go. It's like swimming against the current. It exhausts you. After a while, whoever you are, you just have to let go, and the river brings you home.
—Joanne Harris, *Five Quarters of the Orange*, 2002

My family relaxed by looking north toward Lookout Hill—a view of work done and work yet to do. We faced the multiplying outbuildings and the original big frame barn. The ranch house's long side, with its ample porch, faces away from town and northward toward higher ground. The north porch was the center of activity on long summer evenings. Lookout Hill is a knob three hundred feet higher in elevation than the ranch house and the highest point visible from the house. Kids balanced on the porch's two-by-four railings and adults put their feet up, leaning back on their chairs' back legs. Wooden kitchen chairs and old school bus seats, their covers duct-taped at the seams, served as seating. A narrow-mouthed gallon jug with an inch of milk caught flies. Moths frenzied around the one light bulb until someone turned it off and we sat in darkness, talking and laughing. Northern lights, the wondrous aurora borealis, treated us every few years.

The grassy open area directly north of the ranch house, half a football field in size, was a central square. The Tack Shack framed this space on the east, the barn and corrals on the north, a log cabin and machine shed that my grandfather built on the west, and the fenced yard on the south. The open space allowed a good view of the slope beyond the barn, where we could track livestock movement and often see coyotes. This central area was once a large market garden where Suneson grew rhubarb, asparagus, raspberries, sweet cherries, apricots, and other garden crops to sell in Missoula. My parents found a buried copper still where early homesteaders made moonshine from homegrown rhubarb—yet another North Hills commodity delivered to Missoula. When they took over the ranch, they plowed under the truck farm crops and planted grasses. My parents' identity was as ranchers, not truck farmers. The area became a small pasture for a horse in training, bum lambs, or my 4-H livestock. It is where Blue lay dying.

The North Hills' settled areas speak volumes about life at the margins. The oldest layer we could see from "porch-sitting," as we called it, was the big barn and the chicken house. To an outside eye, the sagging barn and the chicken house's peeling paint looked run-down, but they represent a lifetime of getting by with little and not having time for niceties. Hard work and innovation sustained families and kept enterprises rumbling forward. In contrast to the Randolph homestead, the buildings at Skyline Ranch show newer ways of doing things, even though the old patterns are still visible.

My parents had a passion for cast-off buildings; their scavenged sheds created a newer layer on the ranch's original blueprint. In the 1970s and 1980s, an explosion of buildings changed the ranch's appearance and function. In 1971 my parents dismantled several structures at the defunct Missoula Sawmill on West Broadway, harvesting huge trusses, lumber, and usable wooden panels. My mother single-handedly filled a fifty-gallon barrel with nails she pulled from the reclaimed boards. Hard-core collectors, they never had just one of something they liked. They would find some small shack that someone wanted to get rid of, put a temporary axle under it or load it onto a flatbed truck, and haul it to the ranch. It became a granary, woodshed, or storeroom. It might keep the snow off a few loads of hay or a stack of old snow tires. My aunt Martha and her teen daughter, during an in-between phase, lived in a shed we called the Blue Room for its faded, chipping blue paint. It had electricity but no running water.

For my family, and for many other westerners, a legacy of saving, moving, and reusing buildings persists. Each shed has a story. My grandfather's sister Olive lived on a Swan Valley ranch after coming to Montana from Norway. In 1949 her neighbor wanted to get rid of a log cabin. A $75 receipt dated August 4, 1949, shows the sale to L. G. Kramen, my grandfather, of a log house with permission to haul it out. He took it apart log-by-log, marking each piece for easier reassembly. Then he made multiple trips in his garbage-hauling truck, moving logs to the ranch. At that time people made the eighty-mile trip from Missoula to the Swan Valley over rutted, bumpy dirt roads: getting there and back could take all day. He reassembled the cabin across the ranch house's driveway. We don't know his original intentions, but the cabin was always used as a spare bedroom. I remember sleeping there as a child, napping after lunch with my grandparents, who believed in the early afternoon siesta. For the last fifty years my mom has rented the cabin, often to University of Montana students.

Sometime in the 1980s, Mom spotted one-half of a big metal boxcar parked near the landfill entrance. "Wouldn't that be a great garage for the backhoe!" She bought it for $100 and the owner towed it to the ranch instead of paying the landfill to take it. It still houses the old backhoe. Another six-by-eight-foot storage building was formerly a ticket booth at the Missoula County fairgrounds, its sales window still intact. We call another shack the Biffy Barn, named by my son Rye for its origins at BFI, the former name of what is now Republic Services. When BFI built a bigger and better shop at the dump, my parents paid a mover $600 to pull the old one to the ranch. Salvaged sheds got bigger over time as my parents developed the confidence and skill to move them.

The boxcar phase had a big impact on the ranch. Old Man Suneson made do with a barn and a handful of outbuildings, never dreaming of boxcars rolling up to North Hills ranches. The Northern Pacific Railroad disposed of old boxcars, minus their wheels and undercarriages. Haul them away and they were yours for one dollar. Mom and Dad acquired four during the 1970s. Dad put big axles under each and used a truck to pull it the two miles to the ranch. John and I lived in one. It was our first home, while we attended the University of Montana, for a couple of years after our 1972 marriage.

Our cozy boxcar cottage still rests in the shade of an old apricot tree and a taller Chinese elm at the east edge of the ranch house yard. One long side faces west and one short end faces the Randolphs, as though it could run on a southbound rail. The boxcar is eight by thirty-four feet, about the size of a motor home. The NP had clad the outside with horizontal boards painted its signature brownish red color. We were ahead of our time. Tiny houses are now the rage. Today's trendy recyclers turn shipping containers, which replaced boxcars in the freight industry, into houses.

Teams of railroad track maintenance workers, called gandy-dancers, had long used our boxcar for storage. It had not contained livestock or other smelly shipments. Inside, it had greasy walls and a battered wood floor. The boxcar was one room, except for a floor-to-ceiling wooden tool cabinet built against one long wall, serving as our only closet. We put a big window into the west-facing wall, with views of the ranch house and the sunset. I sewed curtains from strips of upcycled clothing. We cut a hole for a kitchen window facing south. John installed a black Monarch wood cookstove (the only source of heat), guiding its chimney pipe through a new ceiling hole. The kitchen held an upright Hoosier-style cabinet, a drop-leaf table, and a sink in a high wooden counter. We had electricity but hauled water from the ranch house and used one of its bathrooms. Out back, we suspended a fifty-gallon water tank above a small enclosure made of recycled bark-covered wood slabs. We painted the tank black to heat water for leisurely summer showers. Beyond it, marching up the gentle hillside, sweet corn grew higher than our heads, and tomato plants bloomed in our two-acre garden.

We kept a few animals—goats, geese, a milk cow—and felt like homesteaders. I still owned some sheep from my 4-H days. We subscribed to *Countryside and Small Stock Journal*, whose tag line is still "the magazine of modern homesteading." But my first magazine subscription as a newlywed was to *Organic Gardening*, which inspired the huge vegetable patch. We sold produce at Missoula's farmer's market, started in 1972 by the train depot. In the early 1970s we were barely getting by, but like my parents and grandparents before me at the ranch, we did not feel poor. Scott and Helen Nearing, writing from faraway Maine, were our heroes. Their book *Living the Good Life: How to Live Sanely and Simply in a Troubled World* was a manifesto for the organic gardening and hippie back-to-the-land movement of the 1970s.

Other boxcars followed. My dad built the main shop for the ranch in the 1970s from two wooden boxcars. He parked them parallel, about twenty feet apart, and spanned recycled roof trusses, gleaned from the Missoula Sawmill, over them. Dad built walls at both ends and, after pouring concrete to pave the center section between them, had an enclosed central space with boxcar "rooms" on either side. The boxcars stored a mishmash of building materials, restaurant equipment, and chaotic piles from a lifetime of haphazard collecting. The center area held a vehicle or two. A big woodstove made from an old oil drum sat near one corner.

My dad and brother spent many cold winter evenings hanging out in the shop, stoking the fire with scrap wood, tinkering with some old truck or another. Old girly calendars watched over the greasy wooden tool bench that ran across the shop's entire south end. Above them, grimy windows faced south, but the bank into which the building nestled blocked the view of the house and road. The floor was always strewn with sawdust, metal scraps, and dirt clods. A duct-taped ancient recliner orbited somewhere near the woodstove. My dad covered the shop walls with hooks and nails for hanging saws, tire chains, winches, and pulleys. He hung an assortment of old shelves and wooden cubbies on the walls and nailed up old signs and license plates on other walls. At times he tried to stay tidy, but as he got older the shop became more disordered, as did the rest of the ranch's built-up area.

ON AN EARLY SPRING VISIT to Missoula from Michigan in 2005, I witnessed the ranch's increasing chaos during an episode with my mom.

"Here, you take this can of Raid. I've got a shovel." She is convinced that intruders have broken into the shop, so she arms us with weapons. I'm both terrified of the developing situation and amazed at her calmness. In this kitchen, which emphasizes function over form, it's not uncommon to see a can of beans next to a coffee can full of screwdrivers next to a bag of potting soil, so I'm not surprised that she has a shovel handy. I try to convince her to call the sheriff, or at least my brother. She'll have nothing of it. At almost seventy, she doesn't seem the least bit frightened, but mad as hell. In the dark, we head out the kitchen door toward the big shop.

This is more than I bargained for. My dad has been dead for a year and a half. I am here to arrange a permanent return to Missoula, a move planned for later in 2005. It is a tense time. My mother struggles in widowhood, still adjusting to life on her own after a forty-seven-year marriage. A month before my visit, vandals ransacked the shop, a particularly hurtful target since this was the center of Dad's ranch world. My brother had parked his old Chevy Blazer inside, with the shop's huge sliding door padlocked behind it. The thieves didn't break in that way, and the mystery of their entry persists. Once they had the Blazer started, they gunned it forward into the shop bench and then slammed it in reverse to ram the big sliding door. The shop, not tidy when they started, was now trashed. They destroyed large power tools by driving through and over them. Hardware and tools flew everywhere. The big door finally crashed down after enough blows to knock it off its track. The thieves then drove off in the bashed-up Blazer, which the police found the next day a few miles away.

The shop's south-facing windows are partly visible as one drives up the road, and I saw them shining as I drove up the road this evening. When I mention the lights to my mom, she mobilizes. She thinks that the thieves have returned, and she's ready to defend her ground. I'm glad she doesn't go for any firearms.

It's black out, cold and icy. Mom has a flashlight but doesn't turn it on because she wants to stay unseen. We work our way around the house, across the driveway. We stop at the log cabin to tell Mom's tenant about our mission. She'll know that something dire has happened if we don't come back. We creep across the farm road and cross in front of the old chicken house. From

PHOTO 12. The author's mother, Harriet Spurlock, feeding bum calves at Skyline Ranch, 1973. Photo by Donna Erickson. Author's family collection.

there the sneak gets harder. We whisper our plan to peek into the shop windows. She expects to see foul play. My heart races as we half crawl, half slide down the clay embankment. We peek into the window but don't see anyone. She says, "Let's go inside to make sure." Stumbling along the side of the boxcar, we reach the big sliding door. The padlock holds tight, so she unlocks it and we slide the door open a crack. Still nobody in sight. She hollers, "Is anybody here?" Not a sound.

The episode is a false alarm; my brother has simply forgotten to turn off the light. When we get back to her kitchen, she explains that she is still dealing with the police and the insurance company about the break-in. The former never found the criminals, and the latter wasn't convinced there was much new damage. When my mom told me about her interactions with the claims adjuster, I could imagine him tiptoeing in shiny loafers around the shop's disheveled contents. The insurance company eventually paid only a small part of her claim.

After years of being apart from my mother, except for a few days a year, the shop episode reminds me how tough this woman remains. I've rarely seen her cry, other than when her parents died, over a decade apart, and then when her husband died in 2003. She loves animals; I remember her sobs when a Guernsey calf died in 1973.

My mom and her can of Raid remind me that the ranch faces new challenges. Where the issues were once weeds, fire, and drought—natural phenomena—they now include human maliciousness and the inertia of aging. As people get older and pass, gravity takes over. I am realizing that Dad's death unraveled the working ranch. His life was part of the ranch's chemistry. Since I'd been gone for twenty-five years, I did not fully understand the situation. When I came home a couple of times a year, I'd seen the accumulating piles, the unfinished projects, and the loss of focus. With the break-in episode, things felt more precarious. I was used to the haphazard projects that erupted randomly. On impulse, my parents would start a new corral because someone offered them cheap fence posts. But soon the project was neglected in order to finish other urgent tasks, like getting the hay baled or reworking a water trough. Many projects were never finished.

Every time I went to the ranch while I lived away, I fantasized about someday helping clean it up. I longed to peel back the layers of the ranch's history and reveal the original structure, to create order. I'm an organizer at heart, and it pains me to see the ranch deteriorate. Our old boxcar home is full of discarded building materials, broken down furniture, and rusty bedsprings. Although the woodstove and Hoosier-style cabinet we used over forty-five years ago are intact, birds and mice have taken over inside.

My mom was born during the Great Depression of the 1930s, which shaped her worldview and her need to store belongings. She can no longer mobilize to take advantage of a great bargain on a shed. Like many aging people, Mom is now ready to offload instead of acquire. Fifteen years after the Raid episode, now in her eighties, she realizes that Skyline Ranch needs an overhaul. She knows that a lot of stuff has to go.

11

A RANCH'S RUSTY JUMBLE

If it can't be reduced, reused, repaired, rebuilt, refurbished, refinished, resold, recycled, or composted, then it should be restricted, re-designed or removed from production.
    —Pete Seeger lyrics, *Pete Seeger at 89*, 2008

"We'll never have an auction on this place as long as I'm standing!" My mom's ban creates a dilemma: what to do with nearly a century of accumulated equipment and tools at Skyline Ranch now that it's no longer a working cattle ranch. Mom has a worn black and white composition book listing ranch buildings. The tally is thirty-three, including her farmhouse; the log cabin, garages, hay sheds, shop, granary, and storage sheds; and the ranch's 1910 barn. Some buildings are the size of a closet, and others are big enough to house several trucks and tractors. One column of her building matrix is titled "Sorted," with almost no checkmarks yet. There are interesting treasures in nearly all of them, and some contain purchases from auctions I attended as a child. I'm working on cleaning up the sheds, taking stock, and investing myself back into the place—coming full circle after an adulthood outside ranching.

Throughout my childhood in the 1950s and early 1960s, my grandparents took me to farm auctions. My family called the auctions "farm sales," a term that now connotes a real estate transaction more than the selling of old John Deeres. Kids ran around, largely unsupervised, exploring and playing games among the flatbed trailers loaded with chicken feeders, scrap iron, hay hooks, and fence posts. Auction companies or the local 4-H club sold coffee, pop, donuts, and sometimes burgers and hot dogs from the back of a wagon or pickup.

Folks milled around, looking through piles of household belongings arranged across the farmyard or grassy lawn—furniture, small tools, carpets, and appliances. The auctioneer saved the good equipment for later in the day. That kept people hooked as they waited for coveted items to be sold. Meanwhile, they were apt to make other spontaneous purchases. Household items sold in the morning, while tractors, trucks, and even buildings and livestock came in the prime time after lunch. The auction company lined up trucks, irrigation pipe, balers, and plows in neat rows near the barn. The sale was wrapped up in time to get people home for supper.

The auctioneer was a master of timing and crowd control. His rhythmic sing-song kept buyers focused, entertained them and, more than that, cajoled them for the highest dollar.

Five dollar bid, now ten
Now ten, will ya give me ten?
Ten-dollar bid, now fifteen
Now fifteen, will ya give me fifteen?
Who'll give me fifteen?
Fifteen dollar bid, will ya give me twenty?
Twenty, twenty, twenty. This water trough is just like new folks.
Who'll give me twenty?

Going once, going twice, sold.

Fifteen dollars to buyer number twenty-four.

People clustered in front of the auctioneer and engaged in mostly friendly bidding competition. In my early twenties, I fell in love with one of Singer's first electric sewing machines at a farm sale in the Flathead Valley. The black machine with its gold lettering rested in a wooden cabinet with tiny drawers. A middle-aged woman sauntered over, checked it out, and mumbled to me that it probably didn't work and wasn't worth much. But, seasoned by years of farm sales, I knew what she was up to. Of course she bid against me, but I bought the machine and used it for decades.

I remember farm sales as sunny outings along small creeks, beside grassy meadows on gorgeous May mornings. The odors of greasy tools and fresh coffee mixed in the air. My grandparents ventured out to farm sales when the weather was fair, and my time with them was infused with softness and caring.

As a child I was unaware of the melancholy often associated with farm sales. Families held auctions as a result of a farmer's death or illness. A cluster of family members watched from the edge of the throng. Widows preparing to move from the land where they had spent most of their lives watched their china cabinets or washing machines pass into someone else's life. The auctions had an aspect of voyeurism, with people traipsing through the family's belongings, judging the worth of this drop-leaf table or guessing the age of that band saw.

Farm sales provided important community time—a fair atmosphere for kids, but for adults a chance to show respect for a dead neighbor. Being there showed concern and helped the family financially. People could find out what farm equipment was "going for" and socialize with neighbors and friends. A farm sale was a frugal way to obtain farm paraphernalia—from boxes of Ball canning jars to anvils and fencing staples. The collective group of auction-goers knew the value of these items—not the monetary worth in precise terms, but how to use them. They bought items not to decorate the walls of vaulted-ceilinged rooms in a second home, but to make a living in agriculture. The objects could be put back to life to fulfill new dreams. Life continued through these practical pieces of a family's past.

At a sale, my grandfather would become restless late in the afternoon, eager to get back to milk his cows. He would pay up at the table where a woman operated a hand-crank adding machine. He'd then load the smaller items in the trunk of his late '40s Chevrolet sedan and gather me into the front seat. My grandmother's lap was a comfortable place after a day well spent, as the Chevy crunched on the gravel to the ranch. They'd return the next day to haul any big equipment with Grandpa's 1936 International truck.

In a June 1946 diary entry, my grandmother wrote: "We went to sale out at Cunningham ranch. We bought hay rake, mower, pack saddle, plow, keg of staples, barrel of gas, and wheat." Fifty years later, I'm in a ranch shed where some of my grandparents' and parents' farm sale finds landed. When I come across a vintage chicken feeder or rusty cast-iron light fixture, I wonder what farm sale it came from. A hay meadow along the Bitterroot River? A ranch in the foothills of the Mission Range? Or maybe a place near Ovando up the Big Blackfoot? I remember them all.

Now, in 2014, I find a lot to get rid of. My inventory in just one section of the harness shed reads "horse-drawn wagon, boxes of wiring, antique thresher, water heater, seed cleaner, trailer house tires, two nice doors, oak rocker." The list ranges from the functional to the valuable to the beautiful. Some items were all three; others, none of the above. My mother mandates that, for us, any clearance will have to be handled off-site. To her, a farm sale is giving up. It is a defining moment that means things have changed for this family on this land. It signifies an undeniable passing, and she's not ready for that. Unfinished projects are on view for the world to see. The family's successes are visible, exemplified by functional machinery, a hay crop ready to mow, and healthy livestock. But unrealized dreams and personal limitations are on view as well. A life's work comes to this.

I'm the first person to touch many of these things in half a century. My old jeans, sweatshirt, and hiking boots are covered in a fine coat of bird poop. It's late November, but I'm staying warm by working. The respirator mask is uncomfortable, but it protects my airways from the dust and mouse droppings. Little do I know that I'll need to get used to this inconvenience in 2020. I'm shoveling detritus into a garbage can, slowly gaining access to the things stored on the deep, rickety shelves lining two walls of an old shed.

I can hear my mom walking down the road, a ski pole in each hand to steady her legs. "How's it going in there? What are you finding?" She's looking in through the open door from the road, not able to navigate the steep, slippery path up to the door. I point toward the back of the shed. "I've found eighteen ten-gallon cream cans." Mom shocks me by saying, "Eighteen cream cans! We might as well get rid of them." My family does not, in general, "get rid of" anything. When you combine that with the tendency to hoard multiples of specific items, it adds up to impractical, inaccessible accumulations. If you need a door, there are probably a hundred stored at the ranch. It's easier to go to Home Depot and buy one. Mom is now realizing this.

"Is there a rope in there? We can tie it to one of those shelf supports, then I can pull myself up." The woman has grit, cemented by stolid Nordic roots. She wears her long red hair—not graying but faded to auburn in her early eighties—plaited into a practical braid down her back. Her hands are freckled, wide, and strong—hands that have taken her through a lifetime of hard manual labor. As we work together, she tells me where things came from, weaving stories about livestock, neighbors, her parents and, above all—work. Mom knows where she and my dad bought that ornate cast-iron stove, how much it cost, and which truck they used to haul it to the ranch.

Over many days, I make good headway. I sort cast-iron woodstove parts and line them up on a shelf—burner plates, ornate legs, and grates. I separate categories into buckets: garbage, metal recycling, copper recycling, and scrap wood to burn. When I've made enough room, I start new categories: *Sell after cleaning? Does any family member want? What is this? Repurpose?* Far more than a cleaning project, this is a quest. I relish the challenge of separating the things that offer renewal from those that do not.

After repairing, cleaning, and pricing items, I take them to my rented booth in a local antique mall. I'm amazed that people will buy a rusty old bucket that doesn't hold water.

There is a stark difference in how ranchers think of extra stuff, compared with urbanites. Ranchers usually have scrap iron piles, heaps of old fence

PHOTO 13. The author's booth at the Montana Antique Mall, featuring items for sale from Skyline Ranch. Foreground: cream separator, crock and milk can. Barnwood for sale on the back wall. Photo by Donna Erickson.

posts, and other collected materials in case they're needed someday. Why do urban people buy old, rusty junk? I think it's because vintage things allow us to elide time, to follow objects across layered decades. They connect us to memories, experiences, and family. They capture the imagination on the one hand but have practical value on the other. Using, or even displaying, that old bucket keeps us from buying new stuff. William Randolph must have gotten much pleasure from building his whirligig out of scraps lying around at the Moon-Randolph Homestead.

I find good success in selling Skyline Ranch extras, and a dozen cream cans are the first to go. We agree that we will only sell things that Mom, my brother, and I agree on. I start a special account for the items sold from the sheds, a scholarship fund that my mom's grandchildren and great-grandchildren can someday use. But this work is not really about money; it is a creative pursuit. I dig out a 1950s wooden vanity from under a musty tarp. Most people would throw it away, but I think, "Tighten the screws and apply a coat of paint and this will be nice for a little girl's room."

Akin to a farm sale, these projects pull us together. My fifteen-year-old niece helped me one day as I worked at the boxcar where I had lived over forty years ago. It felt like coming full circle; I remember working in the same spot all those years ago, but then I was a newlywed starting my first garden and tending my goats. My mom, niece, and I were hauling away the garbage I'd accumulated cleaning out detritus from the boxcar. We were picking up pieces of glass, wood scraps, and other garbage. I tried to impress upon my niece that "this is about taking pride in the place."

My family connects over work and junk the way other families bond over beach vacations. Many items have invisible fingerprints—hopes, plans, and anecdotes clinging to them. I hear the stories that long-abandoned objects trigger in my mom's memory, and I'm glad to be doing this now rather than when she's gone. In earlier decades she would say, "Oh, that was Mother's," meaning it had to be kept. Now she likes reminiscing about the things we find, and telling their stories helps her release the objects. Unlike farm sale widows, she feels satisfied that the story of acquiring and using an item has been honored. Much of the junk at Skyline Ranch represents dreams and plans that didn't play out, yet telling their stories is like passing along a family album. It lessens regrets.

THE TACK SHACK is the building most like a family album. Located about a hundred feet northeast of the house, this one-room building is a functional and sentimental family hub. My parents moved the twelve-by-twenty-four-foot shed to the ranch in the 1960s. Dad installed a sturdy twelve-foot-long hitching post a few feet from the Tack Shack's front door. This is where we groomed, saddled, trained, and doctored horses. Since the Tack Shack was visible from the north porch, it was a focal point and my parents tried to keep it tidy and painted. Sometime in the 1980s my sons painted it white and yellow, alternating colors on the board and batten siding.

When I was growing up, we kept all horse gear in the Tack Shack. A double-tier rack for saddles and horse blankets lines the back wall, and dozens of hooks, welded from horseshoes, hold bridles, halters, ropes, and har-

PHOTO 14. The author's sons, Rye and Reed, on their pony Cappy in 1981. The Tack Shack is directly behind them; to the right is the boxcar that had become a home nearly a decade earlier. Photo by Donna Erickson.

nesses. One end of the Tack Shack has a counter holding a glass showcase across the entire wall, first used to display candy and cigarettes in my parents' café enterprises. It now holds dozens of ribbons and trophies that my brother and I won for 4-H projects and horse shows in the 1960s. My dad collected hundreds of bits and spurs, which he attached to the rafters with fencing staples. When I walk in, my eyes are drawn upward to the shiny curved metal of old spurs in all designs and sizes. Their rowels—the piece that prods the horse's side—range from the iconic spinning star to the more benign nubbins of English riding spurs. Many of the bits are well over a hundred years old, from gentle snaffles to severe spades. The nomenclature of horse bit designs is as complicated as horse breeds.

Sometime after I'd moved away and the family was riding less, my parents moved much of the good tack to another shed. They left the very old saddles and other relics where they were. The Tack Shack started to become a disheveled museum where antiques accumulated—kerosene lamps, old crocks, animal traps, saddle bags, wooden churns, leather gun scabbards, cast-iron skillets, and more. Clearly my grandparents scrounged many of these items from farm sales in the mid-twentieth century. In 2017 I began the clean-up. I emptied the glass display case to clean out mouse droppings and grime. Some of the tails on the silky award ribbons had been chewed by mice. I sorted, scrubbed, purged, and organized.

My dad used the Tack Shack as a cowboy man cave. He would fire up the Majestic cookstove to heat the small space. In front of the stove sat an old stuffed easy chair with Dad's leatherwork tools nearby. A cast-iron cauldron—two feet deep and three feet in diameter—sat by the wall near his chair. He filled it with harness oil to soak bridles and other leather. Sitting in his easy chair, he'd rub the oil into the leather to keep it soft and supple. Back then the comforting smell of oiled leather enveloped me at the doorway. His last work here was probably in the early 1990s. That cauldron, unused for thirty years when I started cleaning, was more than a foot deep in thick, greasy black oil.

That lovely, oiled leather smell had turned rancid. One September day my husband and I decided to empty the cauldron. Our plan was to put the oil into five-gallon buckets and take them to a hazardous material drop site. As we dragged the sloshing cauldron a few feet outside the door, the odor became worse. I scooped with a big ladle; it was sludgy on the bottom. Suddenly, I started scooping out whole black, slimy mice! I'm not usually squeamish but this was too much; I started screaming and jumped away in disgust. The mice had gotten into the pot, probably to chew on the leather, and couldn't climb back out on the greased surface. They drowned by the dozens and the oily grave preserved them intact.

MY WORK, from the rewarding to the repellant, can perhaps bring new life to Skyline Ranch. My family communicates through work, and by working we begin considering what will happen with the ranch, envisioning a next chapter. By starting to deal with the accumulated odds and ends of generations, we can imagine new endeavors while appreciating the old. Cleaning it up—touching the relics of departed relatives—feels like a huge step forward, not just nostalgia for the past. It's about hope, thinking about future generations, honoring past work while being realistic about new ways of doing things.

Maybe my family won't need an auction, and my mom's wishes will be honored. And many of the objects we find and clean will not be sold quite yet. However, the rusty beauty of some ranch objects can find new homes and renewed uses after Mom has told their stories. Their usefulness has not ended. It is gratifying to pass these objects on, to connect with people who appreciate the beauty and meaning of purchases my grandparents made on sunny May mornings in Montana.

PART 3

FORCES OF CHANGE AT THE EDGE

12

FORCE TIMES DISTANCE

> If you see a whole thing—it seems that it's always beautiful. Planets, lives... But up close a world's all dirt and rocks. And day to day, life's a hard job, you get tired, you lose the pattern.
> —Ursula K. Le Guin, *The Dispossessed*, 1974

Post-hole diggers curse... saddle horses stumble... hay mowers jam... kids moan. Nothing defies ranching on hilly ground so much as rocks. In fact, geology had a lot to do with the entrepreneurship of North Hills pioneers and the hardships they endured. Two of the main activities in ranching are fencing and haying. In these hills, both are about moving rocks. Physics defines work as force times distance, where work measures the energy expended in applying a force to move an object. Much of my childhood was spent applying that force to rocks and hay bales.

Rocks are continually in your way as you're putting in a fence across these steep hills. For today's fence builders, rocks are more of an annoyance, sometimes stopping the automated post driver from getting its thin green metal fence post a couple of feet into the ground. A tractor powers the post pounder, and it usually just pushes the iron in, wedging it around all but the largest stones. Earlier generations had it a lot harder.

Like ranchers across western Montana, North Hills pioneers built fences by hand, with a shovel and a tamping bar. Ray Moon, the first homesteader on the Randolph place, wrote that he built almost two miles of fence during the five years he "proved up" on his land. My grandfather claimed even more mileage. He lodged wooden posts at least three feet into the ground, sinking them below the frost line to prevent heaving in freeze-thaw cycles. He and his neighbors used teams of horses to haul materials, sons or daughters to help string barbed wire, and strong backs to set posts. My mother recalls holding posts as plumb as she could while her dad pounded the top. Crack! He smashed the post, driving it down a few more inches, after he'd swung the twenty-pound sledgehammer in a full circle around his body. Missing would have meant a mangled, broken arm for my mom, but that never happened.

Fencing was punishing work. My grandfather used square railroad ties, ten inches wide and eight feet tall, as corner posts and gateways. Those could not be pounded in. My grandfather dug a deep hole into the dry ground, at least two feet wide, shoveling dirt and rocks out and then dropping the post in. Then he shoveled everything back into the hole. Those rocks, villains on their way out, became allies going back in. Rocks stabilized the post and helped it stay vertical for decades after he tamped them into the hole and wedged them against the post.

Rocks had other productive roles. My grandfather hung large stones from wire on the uphill side of posts, so that over time posts would not tilt downhill. He also used rocks to drape wire into low places. Where a fence crosses a small draw, you'll often see angular stones hanging from the lowest wire in order to pull it down and prevent livestock from squeezing under. And, of

PHOTO 15. Lawrence Kramen pulling a stoneboat loaded with hay in the 1950s. Photo by Mildred Kramen. Author's family collection.

course, the right rock wasn't necessarily at hand. My grandfather hauled it there on a stoneboat.

Stoneboats helped settle the American west, at least in its rockiest regions. Some version has probably been used to move rocks since the Egyptians built the pyramids, and before. Stoneboats are low, rudderless wooden sleds with runners, pulled by horses and now sometimes dragged behind tractors. Farmers and ranchers used them to haul other materials as well—milk cans, hay, and firewood. Ranchers built stoneboats of oak or other hardwoods that stood the abuse of being dragged over uneven, rocky ground. We recently found the disassembled runners from my grandfather's stoneboat in a shed as we scavenged for wood suited to a woodworking project. My parents stored the runners decades ago; hardwood carries a premium in this region of weaker native timber. Front-end loaders and other power equipment replaced the stoneboat for modern fencing.

The North Hills hayfields were also hard-won. Haying is a central activity of family farming in western Montana. "Hay" is not just a noun but a

PHOTO 16. This rock near the Lone Pine was wired to the bottom of a barbed wire fence by Lawrence Kramen in the 1940s or 1950s. The rock helps keep wires low so livestock cannot crawl under. Photo by Donna Erickson.

verb where haying is a discrete ranching season. By around the fourth of July, the fields where we had picked rocks were knee-high in thick emerald-green alfalfa, with its clover-like leaves and small purple blossoms. In Montana's more fertile, irrigated valleys, farmers can harvest three or even four cuttings of alfalfa; we were lucky to get two. Without irrigation, we relied on rain for the alfalfa to thrive. Missoula gets about sixteen inches of rain per year, and we always hoped the usual pattern held—most rainfall in May and June and far less in July. We mowed hay just as the plants were budding out, dry weather permitting, and then raked it into windrows. After the windrows dried for a day or two, my dad baled the hay with a baler pulled behind the tractor.

My grandparents didn't bale the hay but stacked it loosely on a truck or trailer and then hauled it to the barn loft. The pitchfork was the primary implement for moving the hay from the field to the truck. From that humble haying tool, we derived an entire attitude about work in our family—"pitching in."

PHOTO 17. Lawrence Kramen haying with horse-drawn equipment in the hayfield near the house at Skyline Ranch. Photo by Mildred Kramen. Author's family collection.

Everyone was expected to tackle the task at hand, to dig in and help accomplish what needed to be done—to "make hay while the sun shines."

My grandparents were putting up hay by June. My grandmother's diary from 1947 shows that they started on June 6 and finished a first cutting on June 19, all accomplished with a team of horses. She writes on June 7: "Raked hay today and took in to the barn. We got 5 loads in lower field. Ivan [hired man] and Daddy took it up into mow with sling. Ivan mowed lower field across road while daddy and I took in first load."

By the time I was working in the fields, we baled the hay. The main hand tool was the hay hook—one in each hand. Although my dad mowed, raked, and baled hay with patched-together farm equipment, the scenario of gathering hay bales was similar to picking rocks—kids fanned out over the field rolling, pushing, or carrying 60–100 pound hay bales to a trailer behind the tractor. The July heat bore down on us as we heaved and grunted heavy bales onto the trailer, using our knees for leverage. "Bucking bales" was another all-hands-on-deck activity, enlisting any relatives who were available and 4-H kids, whom my parents paid a few bucks for a day's labor. Experienced older kids or adults balanced on the moving trailer as they wove the bales together tightly, stacking the first layer in one direction, then the second layer in the other direction, and so forth for six or eight layers. This "tying" prevented the load from tumbling off on the bumpy downhill ride to the barn. Once there, we dropped one bale at a time onto a noisy gas-powered hay elevator that raised it to the loft.

For haying we wore heavier shoes or boots to crunch over the stubble field. Jeans and long sleeves protected us from the scratchy hay. The camaraderie was the same—pacing our day by how many bales we had gathered, how many trips to the barn, and how many truckloads were left. We enjoyed the reprieve of salami sandwiches at lunch and coolers of pop. Later, my sons Rye and Reed did the same work. Kids were expected to help; the work ethic didn't leave room for negotiation. The family focused together on jobs with clear purposes and tangible results. That work was nearly the same from generation to generation, even though the mechanization changed. Now my mom and my brother have a few head of Charolais cattle, but they buy hay for winter feeding. No haying has been done on Skyline Ranch since the 1980s. Now we fight weeds, not rocks.

Of the roughly one thousand acres in use at Skyline Ranch, only about one hundred were ever cultivated as hay ground. That acreage yielded enough hay to sustain around one hundred cows through the winter— the number that could be grazed on the remaining grassland the rest of the year. We cleared rocks so that haying machinery could work the soil. Horses pulled the stoneboat in my mother's childhood, and a small Massey Ferguson tractor pulled it in mine. I hated the necessary evil of "picking rock." The tractor driver throttles down then methodically chugs back and forth across the field, with the stoneboat lurching behind. A rock the size of a soccer ball, or even a softball, can severely damage a hay mower or combine. Modern rock pickers are machines, advertised to be fast, clean, and efficient. These implements almost look like hay balers, harvesting rocks and swallowing them into their bellies. According to Highline Agricultural

Equipment, their rock pickers are "tough farm hands that stand up to the rough and tumble world of rock picking."

It's a hot day in late May 1968, and little green alfalfa sprigs emerge in clumps across the field. I walk behind the stoneboat, range out fifty feet or so, eyes to the ground, spot a rock, pick it up, and throw it onto the stoneboat. Repeat . . . for hours. Only when we come to a big one—hefty enough that it takes two kids to move it—does the tractor idle for a minute or so, the bored driver waiting while two scrawny teenagers wrestle the rock, digging at it if it's partly buried in the ground. Payment for this tedious labor was by the hour or even by the rock. We counted the rocks in our head as we loaded them, which either eased the monotony or added to it. And the supply was perpetual. Every year the land spit up more rocks in its freeze-thaw cycles. On fields that we cultivated each spring, the plow brought up even more stones.

I've gone out ahead of the tractor, scanning for rocks. I pick up a stone, turn it over in my hands, and wait for the tractor to catch up with me. This one has a pearly band all the way around its middle. Rocks on the North Hills are mostly angular pieces of quartzite, harder than granite, some with interesting quartz bands across them. In contrast to the rounded boulders in nearby Rattlesnake Creek, these rocks are less traveled. Most are not worn and smoothed from tumbling great distances over millions of years through water and ice. In handling thousands of rocks over the years, it is not surprising that you find some interesting shapes. Someone, probably my grandfather, found an unusual "keeper" long ago. It's a rounded rock in the size and shape of a man's foot; we've used it as a doorstop at the front door of the ranch house since the 1940s.

We pile the rocks along the fence line at the edge of a draw, where they settle in next to chokecherry and elderberry bushes. Or we take them to the pit. When my grandparents bought the ranch in 1944, a mysterious crater—about 60 by 110 feet—sank into the hillside a hundred yards above the barn. When I was a kid, nobody ever explained to me why it was there, and maybe I didn't ask. Turns out it is a relic of the Suneson years. Like the Carlsons and Randolphs, the Sunesons also dug for coal, although on a very modest scale.

Ranchers dug poor-grade coal to sell in town and mined clay for brick-making—all sources of diverse revenue. The pit once held a four-foot layer of lignite sandwiched between pumicite and heavy clay. Like the coal at the Randolphs', this was brown lignite, different from that at the Carlsons'. At Skyline Ranch, the coal is three hundred feet higher in elevation and even poorer quality than the Carlsons'. The demand for this low-quality coal dried up in the mid-1930s, so the coal-mining operation had shut down by the time old man Suneson sold to my grandparents. For me, the pit was a place to play—my own little amphitheater. And it was a place to dump stuff—wood to burn, old machinery, and rocks.

Our pit is also a remnant of a brick-making period in Missoula, roughly from 1880 to 1920. It is likely that Suneson, or his contractors, dug the pit not for the coal's commercial value, but to get at what lay under it—a layer of salable clay for brick-making. When Glacial Lake Missoula emptied, it left a twenty-foot clay layer that's now largely gone from the Missoula valley, but is intact in higher places rimming the valley. This clay sometimes slumps on the hillsides. Dr. David Alt, a geologist at the University of Montana, joked that many hillside dwellers might find themselves downhill during an especially wet year.

Like its coal, Missoula bricks are poor quality—soft and porous. Clay was but one of many sources of revenue for the hard-scrabble ranchers in the North Hills. Archie Carlson claims that a Missoula man made plans to market the pumicite from these hills. Pumicite powder is a rough-textured volcanic glass, sometimes containing crystals. The fellow hatched an elaborate scheme to produce an orange-scented hand soap—similar to the abrasive Lava soap that men working with their hands have used for over a century. That dream never materialized.

Other than the pit, there is no lingering evidence of the coal and clay mining era at Skyline Ranch. However, the rocks kept coming, offering our family a perpetual opportunity to bond over physical work. We developed a shorthand for making decisions and devised what people now call "hacks" for tackling a task. Today, people spend good money to attend team-building workshops that teach mission-driven collaboration, focus, and productivity.

Picking rocks, like haying, was about teamwork. Early in the morning or the day before, the adults would decide on the day's activity. Little equipment was needed other than the tractor and stoneboat. My 4-H friends and various cousins showed up from town. We filled jerrycans with drinking water and made bags of Wonder bread sandwiches. Everyone had gloves. Kids wore cutoffs, T-shirts, and flimsy tennis shoes. Dad had the old tractor going, and we all piled onto the stoneboat behind it, savoring the cool morning air and earthy spring smells. Once in the field, we had a sort of radar, no two kids going for the same rock. Joking around and eating together in the heat of the midday sun, we could mentally track how much more we had to do, feeling a sense of accomplishment for a morning's work. Like growing stacks of hay bales, we had tangible evidence of progress in the growing rock piles, even though the hayfield did not look much different at the end of the day.

Regardless of how this land is used in the future, it is unlikely that anyone will be picking rocks by hand. Clay or coal will stay underground. It is possible that hay will be grown and harvested, but not in the foreseeable future. Using the land for scenery or elk habitat will take far less manual labor. And if the land is developed for housing, there will be even fewer opportunities for bonding over hard work.

It is 2007, two years after we moved back to Missoula. My son Reed, almost thirty, strains to budge a stone the size of a small suitcase. We are picking rock in reverse. Reed, trained as a geologist, is visiting from the East Coast. We have driven a ranch truck to the Hundred and Sixty to glean stones for building a path, short wall, and patio at our Missoula home. My grandfather's rock piles are long gone—bulldozed into draws or covered by various land improvement schemes. A contractor hired by my parents plowed this western side of the Hundred and Sixty in the 1990s, in hopes of a few spring wheat crops. This was true sod-busting, since this land had never been plowed. I cried when I first visited from Michigan and saw this tillage, fearing that this was never going to be good crop land and that plowing the native grasses would leave the land vulnerable to weeds. If this land could be irrigated, there might be a chance of success; without it, plowing is folly. The man who planted it on shares, whereby he and my parents would split crop proceeds, piled the rocks in a few four-foot piles near the two-track road. They are a gold mine for landscaping if you put your back into it.

It is a warm September day, the land suffused by a tawny brown that signals summer's end. The meadowlark's soft song contrasts with the clash of rock against rock. This is our fourth trip for stones. To fit the rocks together on-site, we need many to choose from. We search for stones with at least one flat side, turning them over this way and that. They can't be too thick because then we can't lift them. Reed climbs to the top of one pile and throws candidates down for inspection. The quartzite doesn't disappoint. "Wow, look at the blue colors in this one! Do you think we can lift it?" "Here's a good one— it's shaped like Tennessee." We choose angular rocks that will be easier to fit into our garden puzzle. We also find many round-edged stones—flat, oblong pancakes, 6–12 inches in diameter. They are so different from the angular quartzite, and we wonder about their geological story.

As we haul the rocks home, I'm reminded of my forebears hauling coal, rhubarb, and eggs to town from the North Hills. There is a special satisfaction in using materials from our ranch in town. A circle is completed across time and space. In addition to these natural treasures, I take pride in reusing materials that earlier generations kept "just in case we might need it." When the Skyline Ranch kitchen was remodeled in the 1960s, after my grandfather died, my parents removed the original beaded wainscoting in the kitchen in favor of modern paneling. My dad duct-taped the boards into bundles and stashed them in the rafters of a shed. Frugal folks in the North Hills were reducing, reusing, and recycling before it was fashionable. After removing many coats of old paint, we used these in our own kitchen—beautiful inch-thick old-growth native fir and larch.

We'll patiently fit the rocks together as a tribute to the hours of picking rock in earlier times. And the centerpiece at the entrance to our path is a streaked light gray stone that Reed found toward the end of our outing. It's flat and about four inches thick—shaped like a giant human foot. Given the generations of hard manual labor at the ranch, the stone foot is an apt symbol.

13

FIRE ROARS UPHILL

Dead grass is awakened by fire, dead earth is awakened by rain. One life will give way to another, the cycle will begin again.
—Susan Dennard, *Windwitch*, 2016

My grandmother spots the smoke roiling over the ridge as she cans homegrown raspberries, glancing out the ranch house window. Only my grandparents and their youngest daughter are at the ranch on this hot summer day. They panic. They could lose crops or livestock, even their home and ranch buildings. Minutes after seeing the fire on the neighboring hillside, my grandfather's instinct is to protect the property boundary.

Grandpa and my mother, Harriet, run up the fence line that borders the Randolph place. In 1945 she's an eight-year-old girl, long fire-engine red braids waving behind her. She helps her father carry water-soaked rags, hoping to save fence posts from burning. It doesn't work. The fire speeds near them through the fence line. Wildfire travels uphill. Grass fires can rage thirty miles per hour or more, so a person on a grassy hillside is in extreme danger if caught in a fire's path.

"Run home!" shouts my grandfather. He sends his little girl to the wettest, greenest, and now safest place on the ranch—the large kitchen garden—as he swings wet gunny sacks at the flames. "Go to the garden and stay there until I get you!" Harriet sprints. She's running downhill, nearly effortlessly, but her heart pounds in fear. In moments she's through the sheep pasture and squeezes under the fence. Her garden refuge is another minute or two run, just east of the house. Standing in the garden, she sees even more smoke billowing along the Randolphs' ridge and down toward their buildings.

Minutes earlier, the fire escaped northward as a city crew burned a fire line on the front side of Waterworks Hill. Workers went home for lunch while it smoldered innocently. But a strong wind blew in, the fire raced north, then it swung westward off the ridge and into the Randolph ranch. Soon, much of the Randolph place is a wall of fire blazing along the ground. It burns a granary to the ground and destroys a field of ripe alfalfa hay. The flames blacken the pasturelands on the Randolph place, and the family loses grass that would have fed their livestock for the rest of the summer, a loss that will never be compensated. The fire comes so close that it scorches the vines climbing the sides of their house. My grandfather hurries home once the fire invades his land, concerned now about protecting his buildings. But after the fire crosses his property line, it heads north in a path visible from the Rattlesnake Valley, well away from his buildings. Flames lick farther still, nearly to the timber at higher elevations over a mile away—land that my grandparents did not own at that time.

Eventually, Forest Service crews roll up to the ranch with backpack sprayers, trying to fill them at a pond-fed garden spigot, which lacks enough water for them to wage much of an offense. Once the fire progresses to the higher elevations, the crew leaves. Luckily, the fire peters out before it enters the timber. Perhaps the wind dies down or the grass on the steep south slopes does not provide enough fuel.

PHOTO 18. The ranch house at Skyline Ranch with hayfield extending nearly to the house's foundation. This photo was taken in the early 1940s before Mildred Kramen started developing a yard and garden, partly as a fire break. Lawrence and Harriet Kramen on horseback. Photo by Mildred Kramen. Author's family collection.

Although the Kramens saved their buildings and livestock, my grandfather stewed about losing much of the fence line separating his land from the Randolphs, built only the year before. So much back-breaking labor had gone into setting those posts in the rocky soil! My grandmother had more basic worries. In the 1940s the hayfield at Skyline Ranch came right to the edge of the house on two sides. The near-miss of the 1945 fire had a heightened significance for the family's safety.

After that scare Grandma got busy building her own fire line, insisting that she needed a green lawn to separate the flammable hay ground from her home. Pictures from the mid-1940s show hayfields crowding nearly to the foundation of the house. Her diary from June 8, 1946, reads, "I started grubbing alfalfa out in front of the house." Her entries all through June and July of that year report her attempts to eradicate the alfalfa—"digging lawn" and "dug some more." Sometimes she put the hired man to the task. Tucked into her copy of the 1936 *New Garden Encyclopedia* is a scrap of yellowed school paper on which she'd listed the plants she planned to grow—including juniper, arborvitae, columbine, and day lilies. Finally, she had a green lawn and dense Caragana hedge to separate her house from another North Hills grass fire. Decades later, natural resource experts have a term for it—creating "defensible space."

Fire broke out on Waterworks Hill nearly every year in the 1940s and 50s. Children lit firecrackers or played with matches on the hillsides. Motorists tossed cigarettes out windows into the dry grass. The city was building the fire break above the North Side neighborhood on that day in 1945 to help manage that threat. The freeway, constructed through Missoula in the mid-60s, had the unintended consequence of squelching some fire danger. It became a type of fire break.

These hills have burned regularly for eons. Grasses dry out quickly on the thin-soiled south-facing slopes. Fire is intrinsic to the ecology of the Missoula valley and surrounding hills and mountains. What didn't burn naturally, the Native occupants set afire to improve rangeland. Although fire is a natural phenomenon on native grasslands, the changing ecosystem has altered natural patterns. The hills surrounding the valley are no longer natural environments.

While the threat of fire originating from town remains a critical worry, the changing plant ecology of the North Hills exacerbates the problem. Bluebunch wheatgrass, the state grass of Montana, is the dominant native bunchgrass in the Big Pasture, but it is increasingly scarce as weeds crowd out the native grasses. On a November 2010 hike across the Big Pasture, I admire the tall golden bluebunch wheatgrass spikelets that are now seeding out. Smooth and graceful, the stems cast a lovely blue-green color across patches growing two to three feet high. It has not been munched down because cattle have not grazed here in the past few years.

Despite the beauty of the native grass, invasive weeds create the most visible vegetation pattern on the North Hills. Even from the city, the autumn hills show distinct splotches of light and dark brown that interlock like puzzle pieces. The light patches are the blond heads of cheatgrass, a one- to two-foot-tall invasive grass. I pull stickers out of my socks and pant legs after walking across a hillside of cheatgrass, trying to avoid spreading the noxious weed. Cheatgrass can completely alter the ecosystems it invades, replace native vegetation, and change fire regimes. It is extremely flammable; fire spreads much faster in areas infested with cheatgrass. It greens up early in the spring, which is why it was introduced originally, but then it dries out early and becomes pitch-hot fuel. It increases fire intensity and decreases periods between fires.

Dried-up spotted knapweed, another aggressive invader, creates the darker puzzle pieces visible from town. My parents have battled knapweed with herbicides for the past twenty years, using federal cost-share money to hire weed spraying from the ground and from the air. They won particular battles but are losing the war. Even so, there are hopeful signs. In those dark knapweed patches, closer inspection finds good bluebunch wheatgrass thriving within the weeds. The lack of grazing gives the native grasses a reprieve—a chance to let deep roots regenerate and strengthen. However, the real concern is that leafy spurge is starting to spread into the Big Pasture. This region's most insidious weed, it is immune to grazing and most chemical treatments. The entire face of Randolph Hill, much of the Carlson place, and certain areas of Skyline Ranch are monocultures of leafy spurge, with its deceptively pretty yellow-green blooms covering the spring hillsides where wildflowers once bloomed. The more you pull leafy spurge, the worse it spreads, due to the plants' vast connections of underground rhizomes. And once burned, leafy spurge rapidly regenerates new shoots from the intact root system.

Some native plants persist. I walk through small patches of good native grasses and forbs that are trying to hold on: rough fescue, Idaho fescue, rubber rabbit brush in bloom, western wheat grass, and needle grass. Bluebirds flit along the barbed-wire fence, although there are far fewer than when I was young.

Weeds like knapweed, cheatgrass, and leafy spurge have created the most dramatic ecological change in the North Hills over the past forty years. The proximity to town makes the ranches more susceptible to weed invasions since disturbances on suburban neighbors' properties invite weeds that colonize aggressively. The city was so concerned about the management problems associated with outbreaks of leafy spurge and spotted knapweed that it considered selling the Moon-Randolph Homestead in 1998. Riverfront land seemed more desirable than fighting the uphill battle of weed control.

The city remained committed to the Homestead, partly through an innovative solution to weed control. Leafy spurge is a tasty morsel for sheep, which grazed the hillsides of the Homestead and Mount Jumbo for a dozen years. A Mexican sheepherder tended a flock of 400–600 ewes and lambs, with a few goats mixed in. His campo (old-time sheep wagon), guard dogs, and horse were a popular sight as the sheep moved across the hills overlooking Missoula in search of good weed patches. Getting the sheep to the hills became a community event, as the rancher herded his sheep nine miles from his ranch west of Missoula, through town, and into the North Hills. Immigration issues, specifically the requirement to live in housing with a foundation, eventually prevented the herder from working in Missoula, and the sheep no longer graze these hills.

Without the sheep, the spreading weeds are desiccated in August, increasing the chance of human-caused wildfire. Midsummer fireworks are a particular danger, as are motorized vehicles. The catalytic converter on a vehicle can reach temperatures over 1000 degrees Fahrenheit. A pickup can ignite a grass fire when its underside brushes over the tall grass. Therefore, fire danger prevents even normal travel around the ranch. It is far too dangerous to drive on the two-track dirt roads that have four- to five-foot grasses crowding between the tracks. In addition to the dry, weedy landscape, topography makes the North Hills vulnerable to careless activity at the edge of town. When fire ignites in bone-dry grasses on the south-facing Randolph Hill, it heads uphill toward Skyline Ranch.

It's the late 1960s, on a hot, dry August day. A small fire smolders on Bill Randolph's land above the North Side. Someone in town phones to tell us the hill is on fire. They know the fire is invisible to Bill and to us. After Bill doesn't answer his phone, they try ours. The houses and barnyards of Skyline Ranch and the Randolph place are less than a quarter of a mile apart, angling downhill from both houses, with the Randolphs' access road carved into the bottom. From the kitchen we look across our hayfield to Bill's barn, orchard, house, and hayfields, making it easy to see him as he follows his team of horses, Pat and Babe, raking hay. My parents send me running to tell him his hill is on fire.

There is not enough time to catch and bridle a horse and then maneuver through gates and other obstacles. It is a short distance, but a difficult route. I am fast and tough at fifteen. I race across our hayfield, down the steep bank to his road, through hawthorn, chokecherry, and service berry bushes that whip and scratch at my bare legs below my cutoffs. At the foot of the bank, I scramble back up through patched-together gates, across the orchard, through more makeshift gates, and out into the open sunlight of the hayfield. Luckily, I'm familiar with the quirks of each latch and chain.

Bill and his horses are trudging across the uppermost part of his field. Out of breath and anxious, I strain to catch up. Bill is perched on the metal seat above the rake's tines. There is just enough noise from the rake and the horses' harnesses that he doesn't hear me hollering until I am right alongside his rake. I finally get his attention. "Whoa there," he hollers to the team as he pulls the reins up short. "There's a fire over the hill!" I shout. He takes it in stride, as it has happened so often and nothing ever seems to rile him. But he moves fast—for him. He takes his team to the barnyard and loads his old pickup with a shovel and gunny sacks for fighting the fire. He drives up over the hill as I walk home. By the time he gets to the fire, a city firefighting crew has squelched it.

Bill protected his land from all sides, calmly and deliberately. Like the native grasses, he was deep-rooted and resilient. And he clearly had an appreciation for both the utility and beauty of the land. His April 21, 1956, diary entry, a few months after his mother Emma's death, illustrates the crescendo of color as North Hills wildflowers burst forth. "Everything is most beautiful out of doors. Ideal growing weather and the grass and wildflowers are sure showing what they can do. The yellow sunflowers (we call them), yellow bells, blue bells, Johnny jump up, and many others are sure in abundance along with the pink flowers up on the ridge." In 1956 many more wildflowers and native bunchgrasses thrived on these hills than do now. Weeds were starting to establish, but the native ecosystem was in fairly good shape.

Those pink flowers that Bill wrote about on the ridge were surely bitterroots, blooming close to the ground in dry, rocky, exposed locations that are inhospitable to any but the toughest plants. The Montana state flower is the perfect symbol for the tough Montanan. The plants put out their green

FIRE ROARS UPHILL / 159

tendrils and reach for the sun when it is still freezing in early spring, and the flowers bloom in early June to early July, with 12–18 elliptical petals forming a flower about two inches across. It is amazing that the green, succulent leaves form a kind of star cluster on the ground and then completely disappear before the flower blooms. The flowers look like they've been set loose and strewn over the hillside.

The wildflower show in the North Hills, though diminished over the past few decades, has a particular Missoula following. Michael Moore, a reporter for the *Missoulian*, wrote about Waterworks Hill: "Some dismiss the hill as lumpy and dull, but it's actually an organic form of subtlety dressed up as landscape. It's a thing seen best in its details, and they are at their illuminating best in the springtime." Wildflowers on Waterworks Hill circle the color spectrum—blue lupine, purple larkspur, pink shooting star, red Indian paintbrush, yellow-orange arrowleaf balsamroot, yellow buttercup, and hairy golden aster—all on a bed of greens and punctuated with white accents of yarrow. My favorite is the arrowleaf balsamroot; like Bill Randolph, we called them sunflowers. Nearly three feet tall in places, the showy blooms covered the hillsides in splashes of gold at the highest elevations of Skyline Ranch. Randolph Hill was often so intense with lupine the blue tint was visible from the valley floor.

The scattered ponderosa pines high on the ridge of the Big Pasture are also visible from town. It is remarkable that this wooded ridge has not burned in my family's time. The ranch is mostly grassland, with about one hundred acres of timber and another one hundred acres of grassland with old ponderosas in a sparse park-like pattern, almost all at the highest elevation. The trees show evidence of fires that burned across it a hundred years ago. The only recorded fire through the timber between Grant Creek and the Rattlesnake took place in August 1919 and raged north of the Big Pasture. A landowner in the Grant Creek area let a fire get away from him. He started the blaze to drive away domestic sheep grazing near his property. The fire quickly moved east through the timber of the lower Rattlesnake and burned all the property in Sawmill, Dry, Spring, and Curry Gulches north of Skyline Ranch, destroying four ranch houses. There was so much ill will toward the perpetrator that his life was in danger, according to Forrest Poe, writing in his memoir *Born in Rattlesnake Canyon.* At the end of the twentieth century, with diligent fire suppression, this timber was overgrown, with extensive dead fuel for a fire that, luckily, did not come. My family contracted with a logger to thin the timber in 2000, averting a disastrous wildfire.

At higher elevations, native shrubs also contribute to the floral show, with the spring blossoms of chokecherry, elderberry, serviceberry, mock orange, and plum. Snowberry forms a thick shrubby cover for a variety of wildlife and produces perfectly round white berries in early fall. It forms irregular clumps here and there—key places for birds like lazuli buntings and warblers. Northern orioles nest in the small trees that are mixed within the shrub patches. It also hides carnivores. On a 2014 trip up to The Top, we were shocked when my mom's dog Blue ran ahead of the truck and scared a mama wolf out of a patch of snowberry. After running a couple of hundred yards, she turned and chased Blue. We quickly called Blue into the rig; the wolf probably had a den of pups hidden in the snowberry. People have used snowberry for protection too: Nez Percé Indians wrapped its branches around their cradleboards to keep babies safe from ghosts.

Every Memorial Day, Missoulians decorate graves in the county cemetery with geraniums and mums from local nurseries. The leafy old cemetery is a quiet refuge in an industrial area bordered by the railroad tracks, a plywood plant, and the base of the North Hills. Some of us mark graves with flowers that hold more personal meaning. Lilacs are usually just blooming in Missoula around Memorial Day, and homemade lilac bouquets are sprinkled throughout the cemetery. My family tradition is to pick wildflowers— arrowleaf balsamroot, lupines, and yarrow—to decorate graves. We put them in old pickle jars and decorate family plots, which have splendid views of the North Hills.

In 2008 it was a wet spring with a spectacular wildflower show. At Skyline Ranch grasses are tall and healthy after the spring rains. For nearly a decade, cattle have had only seasonal use of the place, with a local veterinarian paying my mother to pasture his cattle there in the warmer months. They don't even make a big dent in the good grass, now bone dry in the August heat. My mother is in her late seventies, and she worries obsessively about a catastrophic fire on Skyline Ranch—a visceral fear from her childhood. Fire danger remains a part of her life.

A ten-year drought continues to parch western Montana in 2008. The summer is the hottest on record, with eleven days in July over 100°. The governor declares the county a drought disaster. As the temperatures climb, my mom worries that someone will drop a cigarette and catch the hills on fire. Grasses are crisp. Water in the draws dried up many weeks ago. Her water-tank trailer is loaded and ready. Holding three hundred gallons of water, it can be pulled to a grass fire behind a pickup, but it's unlikely that she can respond in time. Will she be home when it starts? Will she be able to get the trailer pulled to the right spot in time? Will three hundred gallons of water be enough? All are unlikely.

As another fire season peaks that year, the City of Missoula has closed Waterworks Hill to hikers, and the temperature climbs in tandem with my mother's worry. This year the ranch is again spared from catastrophic fire. By late September, rains come, my mother is again relieved, and the water wagon is parked for the season.

The native ecosystems of the North Hills are compromised—by more than a century of agriculture, mining, and other non-Native human endeavors. Altered ecosystems change livelihoods, heighten natural disaster risks, and strain relationships between North Hills ranchers and urban neighbors. Fire is one of the pressures that define how rural and urban neighbors relate. Even in the 1940s the North Hills ranches differed from those away from development and towns; the urban-rural tension, so prevalent later in the twenty-first century, was brewing even in the mid-twentieth. Now, the places we intend to conserve are more vulnerable than ever, not only to development but to natural processes like fire at the urban-rural interface.

I'm returning to the ranch house after my long November hike in 2010. Sixty-five years after the 1945 fire that triggered my mom's sprint, I run my hand along a blackened post at the gate separating the sheep pasture and hayfield. The post is pitted and scarred, with one linear gouge burned away. It is a survivor of the 1945 fire but is holding strong where my grandfather sank it. The post is a reminder of North Hills threats, exacerbated by the changing natural history of the region. It is also an apt metaphor for tenacious North Hills ranchers.

14

SHOOT, SHOVEL, AND SHUT UP

A farm is a manipulative creature. There is no such thing as finished. Work comes in a stream and has no end. There are only the things that must be done now and things that can be done later. The threat the farm has got on you, the one that keeps you running from can until can't, is this: do it now, or some living thing will wilt or suffer or die. It's blackmail, really.

—Kristin Kimball, *The Dirty Life: On Farming, Food, and Love*, 2010

Clanging bells alerted us to panic in the sheep pasture. On a warm summer day in 1969, a German shepherd massacred the sheep in minutes. The dog was running alone when he cornered my herd of fifty registered Hampshires. They were grazing in the sheep pasture east and uphill from the house. Early that spring I had placed bells on several ewes so that if the herd started running in fear we would hear the commotion. By the time we got to them, a dozen sheep were splayed out on the ground, some alive but bleeding heavily, others already dead with their throats gashed. The dog had maimed some so badly that they had to be killed. The bold canine stood on the ridge looking back at his killing field.

As my mom and I tended to the injured sheep, my dad followed the dog as he meandered over the hill toward the Rattlesnake Valley, down through what was then a horse ranch, into a subdivision, and to its home. My dad could see the house to which the dog returned. After we herded the traumatized sheep to the corral and cared for the injured, my parents drove to that house. This was not the first encounter of this type for my parents. Several times we had traced dogs to their doorsteps. They knocked politely and the dog's owner came to the door. As it turned out, this conversation was familiar to the German shepherd's owner too.

Dogs roamed freely and often in the 1960s through 1990s, north over Randolph Hill from the North Side neighborhood or from the Rattlesnake Valley to the east. From either direction, it takes big, strong dogs mere minutes to get to Skyline Ranch, only a mile away as the crow flies. German shepherds, Labradors, and malamutes cover long distances quickly, and those breeds tended to be the worst. They chased anything that moved but narrowed in to terrorize vulnerable livestock. We lost sheep, newborn calves, and chickens. They returned if not stopped the first time; once dogs tasted blood, they seemed addicted to recreational killing. Predatory instincts kicked in when the dogs ran in packs. More than once we were told at a dog's doorstep, "I only let my dog out for a half hour. He couldn't have gotten that far and bothered anyone!" They had no idea of the ground their animal could cover in a half hour nor his capacity for carnage. Sometimes there was blood still dripping from the dog's muzzle.

This owner was different. He knew his dog's capabilities and that his pet had an inclination to chase livestock. In fact, the dog had killed before and had gotten away with it. This motivated the owner to buy insurance for an incident like this. He knew that my parents had the legal right to have the dog put down, and he pled for his pet's life, claiming the insurance company would pay for the lost sheep and that the dog would not roam freely again.

My dad agreed since it was our only hope of recovering the animals' value. We feared that we had not seen the last of this dog though, and we vowed that next time we would shoot him. The insurance company paid the claim, and we never saw that dog again.

I overheard my parents mention "shoot, shovel, and shut up," also known as the 3-S treatment, a common way to deal with predators in rural areas. One day my dad witnessed a dog chasing Bill Randolph's goats. Something scared the dog and it started fleeing toward town. Bill emerged from his front door with a rifle, took one shot, and dropped the dog in its tracks. Although 3S is a legal solution to stop marauding dogs, rural landowners sometimes illegally kill and bury wolves or other endangered species, and even sick livestock (such as those with mad cow disease). While 3-S is an unfortunate practice, I understand its use when it comes to killer dogs. It goes with the territory when ranching near an urban area. Missoula is a dog town; perhaps the majority of households own dogs, and the city has ample public land for dog walking, including a "bark park" by the Clark Fork River. The *Missoulian's* classified ads regularly list dogs being given away. I cringe when I read "needs a place to run." It is an agonizing outcome when a dog needs to be put down for killing livestock; ranchers find it best to kill the dog, bury it, and keep quiet.

In Montana if a rancher sees a dog harassing his livestock, he is legally justified in killing the dog with no compensation to the dog's owner. This includes what ranchers call "worrying" livestock—making them nervous and skittish, causing them to bunch up or run helter-skelter. The rancher may also notify the dog owner of her dog's behavior and she has twenty-four hours to put the dog down. If she does not comply, the livestock owner can notify a law enforcement officer, who will intervene. Ranchers are entitled to recover damages from the dog's owner, including the value of the animal, veterinary fees, and other expenses.

Coyotes kill livestock, too, but cause far less trouble than dogs from town. They kill an animal, eat part of it, then leave. For dogs, it is a blood sport. Working as a pack, they can corner a herd of sheep where two fences angle together, then rush through them, slashing throats. Or the dogs hamstring the sheep from behind, gouging out whole chunks of a hind quarter then moving on to the next victim. While far fewer dogs roam unattended now than several decades ago, more people hike with their dogs, often illegally off-leash. The herder who once fanned his weed-eating sheep out on Randolph Hill lost several sheep every year to domestic dogs. Often the owners were slowly hiking uphill as the dogs sprinted ahead, so owners didn't always witness the attacks.

"Shoot, shovel, and shut up" is an emblem for the colliding values of ranchers and their urban and suburban neighbors. When growing towns encroach upon traditional ranches and farms, disparate views of open land clash—a practical, utilitarian view, reflecting ranchers' experiences of eking out a living under difficult circumstances, versus a desire for empty space for dogs to run and people to recreate in. Generally, people's appreciation for open space is positive. They help protect it if they love it. They see it daily from their homes, become intrigued by it, and feel some sense of ownership. However, inappropriate behavior from a few people sometimes follows from that appreciation. North Hills landowners have developed a siege mentality over many decades, due to constant problems not only with dogs but with humans.

People lack the easy and swift access of dogs, but they still trespass indiscriminately and sometimes cause as much, or more, damage. Would you walk into someone's backyard, have a picnic, cut some shrubs down for a small fire, and leave your garbage? Probably not—but that behavior is commonplace on ranchland. Some people clearly think that these hills are "empty" and that they are open to the public. Open space seems anonymous without the immediate cues that someone lives there, owns it, cares about it. If people don't see a house, they might not recognize physical boundaries, and fences don't have much meaning.

With the North Hills' proximity to the landfill, garbage is a recurring issue. Some Missoulians drive to the landfill on Coal Mine Road and, finding the landfill closed for the day, dump their trash by the side of the road leading to the ranch. More than once, my mother held her nose and hoisted flimsy bags of kitchen waste, dirty diapers, and other flotsam into the back of her pickup. She looked for discarded mail, scanning for a consistent address on dirty, crumpled envelopes. Mom then drove to that address and dumped the garbage onto the lawn, just as it had been dumped in her "front yard."

Missoulians arrive in the North Hills by all means—on foot, bike, horse-back, motorcycle, four-wheeler, and 4-wheel-drive pickups. They bring dogs, guns, fence-cutters, matches, chain saws, and booze. They ignite campfires when grass is crispy in August heat, build lean-to shelters in the woods, and shoot toward cattle. It is unusual to circle Skyline Ranch and not see evidence of a campfire or a pile of empty beer cans. Motives vary—most trespassers are harmless, simply out for a Sunday stroll. But if landowners let them roam, other people mistakenly think that access is permitted, and problems multiply. One trespasser began cutting trees to build a log cabin on our land. In the 1970s a series of reported UFO sightings on neighboring property enticed trespassers watching for extraterrestrials. One winter an unfortunate fellow froze to death, at the far northern edge of the ranch, as he tried to walk across our land. Drunk, he had parked in Sawmill Gulch and decided to walk to town from there. The search and rescue workers found him the next day, caught in our barbed-wire fence.

Whether hunting, dog walking, hiking, or stargazing, many trespassers, when confronted, claim they did not know they were on private land. Most people don't cross onto private land at a gate where a *No Trespassing* sign is posted, but crawl through a barbed-wire fence somewhere between gates. Are people obligated to know where they are and whether they're on private or public land? A western code of conduct says they are, but that's not the case everywhere. In European countries, "rambling" on private land *is* an accepted practice. The United Kingdom, for example, remains walker-friendly, with the countryside full of signed and mapped footpaths. Well-maintained trails criss-cross private land in the countryside, and people know what is permissible. Private property rights have a different meaning here, and trespassing is illegal. One fall day, a young man strolled toward me along the ridge of the Big Pasture. When he got closer, I informed him that he was trespassing on private land. He became defensive and replied, with no hint of a British accent, "But in England anyone can walk through anyone's land." After a pregnant pause I explained, "Yeah, but that's four thousand miles away and is irrelevant here."

Signage helps somewhat. Montana law requires landowners to paint a "post, structure, or natural object with at least 50 square inches of fluorescent orange paint" with *No Trespassing* in order to legally keep people out. They can access private land only with explicit permission if signs are posted. These notices must be at each gate or natural point of access to the property. However, the bright orange *No Trespassing* sign pierced with bullet holes is a Montana cliché. Over the years, North Hills ranchers have posted hundreds of *No Trespassing* signs. When not shot at, the signs are ripped down, defaced, or ignored.

For ranchers, the fence is one key to protecting their livelihood. Six miles of perimeter fence delineate Skyline Ranch as private land. For Missoulians living so tantalizingly close to open hillsides they can see from downtown or from their front door, that fence creates only a minor obstacle. Some just don't understand the meaning of a fence line and crawl through. Others are less innocent. Vandals with wire cutters indiscriminately cut fences on public and private land just for sport. In 2002 someone snipped barbed wire on twenty-five sections of fence separating the city-owned Randolph Homestead from private land. They deliberately cut close to the fence posts, perhaps knowing a thing or two about fencing. It is far more difficult to mend wire if it's cut at the post than if it's cut between the posts.

The ranchers of the North Hills are notorious for chasing trespassers off their land. Sometimes both trespassers and landowners carry guns. The Skyline Ranch hillsides provide good winter range for elk, and elk are magnets for hunters trespassing on private land. The law requires every hunter to obtain the landowner's permission before hunting on private property, regardless of whether *No Hunting* signs are posted. Every fall my mother fields dozens of calls from hunters asking to hunt on her land. Relatives she didn't know she had call to check in on her. "And, oh, by the way . . . can I just go up on the hill this weekend and fill my elk tag?"

In general, hunters know where they are. They use maps, but modern technology equips today's hunters to be far better oriented than those of previous generations. Nearly all use GPS and other digital devices for location-finding. Their training includes the geography of the hunt, and they usually respect private property. However, some choose to ignore ownership distinctions. Many years ago, my mom checked the cattle near daybreak on the first day of hunting season. On horseback about a mile from the house, she encountered a man, woman, and teenage boy, each carrying a big-game rifle. Polite, but direct, she approached them about trespassing. After all, they had loaded guns and she had only a horse. The woman claimed, "We came up here to see the sun rise."

My grandfather fed his family elk and deer he hunted in what is now the Rattlesnake Wilderness, far north of the ranch. He rode a horse from the ranch, leading a pack horse, to hunt for days at a time. In the 1940s and 1950s, elk did not range as far south as the ranch in the fall, like they do now. By the 1980s thirty to forty elk had shifted their winter range to the North Hills. Then, in 1996, a particularly bad winter pushed the Rattlesnake elk herd south, and they began wintering in the North Hills every year. They began losing their instinctive migratory behavior, arriving earlier in the fall and leaving later in the spring. The herd exploded to 450 head in the 2000s, and now it is not uncommon to see a herd of 200 head grazing on the south-facing slope of the Big Pasture. None of the North Hills ranchers allow unlimited hunting on their lands, but they do let a few friends and family members hunt. Wildlife advocates accuse them of "harboring" elk, the phenomenon of creating a private game reserve that attracts elk, from which the owners can hand-pick a big bull for the freezer. But in the North Hills, the family-only mandate is more to avoid negative consequences—uncontrolled vehicular access, stray bullets near houses, scattered trash, and gates left open.

For a few hunters in the Rattlesnake Valley, a grazing elk herd just above their houses is just too much to resist. A bad case of buck fever can lead to problems. One snowy day in late fall, two men took their young sons up to the east side of the Big Pasture after watching the elk graze above their houses. My brother caught them after they'd killed two big bulls. He called my mom and the police, both of whom arrived on foot at about the same time. Mom hiked over a mile from her house; two young policemen walked in from the Rattlesnake, wearing slick-soled loafers in a foot of snow. The hunters were

SHOOT, SHOVEL, AND SHUT UP / 169

cooperative and contrite. What they really wanted were the racks for their sons. Mom had to decide whether she wanted to bring trespassing charges against them, but since they were neighbors, she was reluctant to do so. They reached a compromise: the hunters kept the racks without penalty, my brother and the hunters each kept some of the meat, and they donated the rest to the Missoula Food Bank.

"Good fences make good neighbors." People across time, languages, and cultures repeat this proverb. It's hard to know how it originated. Its common modern English usage seems to spring from Robert Frost's poem "Mending Wall," published in 1914. It has become a part of the Code of the West.

Fourteen states, including Montana, have an Open Range Law, which means that if you do not want cattle or other livestock on your property, it is your responsibility to fence them *out*. It is not the responsibility of the rancher to fence livestock *in*. The open range concept dates back to the 1800s, when cattle barons let large herds roam over public land and any private land that wasn't fenced. One summer in the 1990s a neighbor in the Rattlesnake called to complain about a stray bull. The man owned a big new house on forty acres just across our eastern fence line. When my mom went on horseback to retrieve the bull, it was tromping around in the man's empty swimming pool. The homeowner was livid. He threatened to involve his attorney, hollering at Mom about suing. She didn't argue with him but simply rounded up the bull and herded it home. She knew the law was on her side and, in fact, nothing came of it. It was the homeowner's responsibility to fence the bull *out*.

Despite what the law allows, western Montana ranchers do not want their livestock roaming freely. As a practical matter, they fence their livestock in, and neighbors are responsible for helping each other maintain existing fences. The rule is this: neighbors are to meet at the midpoint of the fence line facing each other. Each person maintains the fence portion that is on his or her right. But rarely does this scenario happen when the rancher's neighbor is an exurban accountant who owns twenty or forty acres and no cows. Sensitivity over fences goes far beyond legal obligation. Neighbors show respect for one another by keeping livestock fenced in and not letting their cows eat the neighbor's hay or their bulls breed the neighbor's cows. But as the North

Hills become surrounded by suburban developments, fences no longer have that neighborly quality. They are meant to keep cattle in, but also to keep people out.

Like most people, I am conflict averse. It is painful to witness the issues that surface between North Hills ranchers and their neighbors. The forces that shape this marginal rural place are rooted in diverse values that change over time and across different groups of people. While the connection of these hills to Missoula has long been important, the relationship has changed.

Two clashing views meet at the North Hills fence lines. There were more shared values and expectations between Missoula residents and their rural neighbors in the 1930s, '40s, and '50s. Missoulians were not so many generations removed from the farm. In my grandfather's time, it is likely that people on the North Side often knew the ranch families and understood what was appropriate—not trespassing, asking permission, keeping dogs at home, and hunting on public lands. Over time, ranchers became less connected to the neighborhoods near them and more defensive about urban neighbors.

Ranchers at the urban-rural fringe who want to keep their land intact and working face a range of challenges, many of which stem from values, experiences, and attitudes that differ from those of their urban neighbors. Ranchers try to make a living and come to it with practical blue-collar values. They feel the same sense of privacy, ownership, and security as someone does for their house in town. But instead of one house to watch over and protect, they are trying to keep hundreds of acres safe from dogs, fire, and other threats. Their urban neighbors value the land for other reasons. They love the landscape and may simply not know that they can't have access and that their dogs can't run free. Only by understanding the perspectives of ranchers and townspeople—people who care for the North Hills but have etched their marks in different ways—can it be possible to consider a future that merges these values and protects the land's inherent qualities and ranchers' livelihoods.

SHOOT, SHOVEL, AND SHUT UP / 171

15

THE VIEW FROM HERE

What you see and what you hear depends a great deal on where you are standing. It also depends on what sort of person you are.
—C. S. Lewis, *The Magician's Nephew*, 1955

I am conflicted about scenery. The view complicates life in the North Hills. While the hills' beauty is important to my attachment to the place, scenery represents the gulf separating practical rural landowners from their city neighbors.

Theodore Roosevelt said, "There is nothing more practical than the preservation of beauty, than the preservation of anything that appeals to the higher emotions of mankind." Landscapes create our memories, ambitions, and values. We relate to land in all kinds of emotional, sensory, even mystical ways. Views over the North Hills' gently rolling hillsides and pine-stitched ridges form visceral aesthetic ties. I love seeing the Big Pasture ridge line from different Missoula vantage points. Each day as I drive or bike north over the Clark Fork River, the view shifts with the weather and the season. I may wake on a late October day and from my Missoula home see snow dusting the North Hills, even as city streets are dry. On an early April morning I see the hills draped in fog, almost hidden from the valley floor, with a grassy knob peeking out from the west and a timbered ridge line partly visible above it. Just a couple weeks past the spring solstice, the hills' usual brown tone is tinged with green. Later in summer, wildfire smoke blurs the air, but the rounded North Hills ridges create a compass to the north.

My family appreciates the views—both from and toward the North Hills. For me, the visual sense is especially keen since, as a landscape architect, I learned to appreciate and analyze the components of aesthetic scenes—line, form, texture, and color. In recent years we have gone to The Top not to chase cattle or check fences but to enjoy the view. It is a deeply held tradition. Just as some people always take visitors to a special museum or natural area, we take them to The Top. Since the 1960s we have watched as houses crept up the South Hills across the valley, where their occupants enjoy spectacular views toward the North Hills and the Rattlesnake Wilderness. We decry neighbors who build on nearby ridgetops so they get spectacular views 24/7. People of earlier eras knew better than to build atop ridges, with the extra expense, wind exposure, and environmental disturbance from road building and other infrastructure.

From a distance the North Hills appear serene and static. They form a calm buffer between people strolling past Higgins Avenue shops and mountain lions prowling the Rattlesnake Wilderness. In the early years of World War II, Fort Missoula, on the city's south side, became one of many internment camps holding people of Japanese descent, including U.S. citizens. Despite the tragic violation of American civil liberties, detainees called the camp Bella Vista—Beautiful View. Their main view from the Fort was toward the North Hills and the mountains beyond.

PHOTO 19. The North Hills from Pattee Canyon on Missoula's south side. Mount Sentinel is in the foreground, City of Missoula in the center, and the North Hills in the background. The Rattlesnake Recreation Area and Rattlesnake Wilderness are in the far background to the north. Photo by Donna Erickson. Author's family collection.

The North Hills area is a pivot point, an edge, a place where the city and wilderness nearly collide and where small areas of farm and ranch land separate them. Edges are often contested. The North Hills is part of a larger edge, or ecotone, defined in ecology as a transitional zone between two communities with distinct plant communities and physical characteristics, in this case forest and valley lake bed. The North Hills' bluebunch wheatgrass and fescue grassland are edge species, transitional between the lower mixed-grass prairie and the montane/subalpine grasslands higher in the forest habitats. The influence of two bordering communities is known as the edge effect; many plant and animal species thrive only in these edges. Missoulians thrive there too.

People are drawn to edge places, whether it's a riverbank, meadow perimeter, or hilly overlook. The North Hills have been a popular walking destination over the last thirty years. People can clamber up from Missoula's flat lake bed and enjoy spectacular views of the mountains, sunsets, and the city. Over the last ten years, use has intensified since hikers have an uninterrupted route all the way from the Clark Fork River to the Rattlesnake Wilderness. Numbers of trail users are not going to diminish.

Hiking from Missoula up into the hills was not a pastime in the 1940s and '50s. The hiking craze began in the 1960s and has steadily grown. Now people want open space, seeking something lost in an urban environment. But open space is an elusive concept on its own. I've spent much of my professional life exploring its meanings, methods, and outcomes. For planners, open space protection aims to preserve views, agricultural land, recreational spaces, water resources, wildlife habitat, and non-motorized transportation corridors. Those goals can be at odds with one another, creating tensions and challenges.

Starting in the 1970s, the City of Missoula has been trying to preserve open space, particularly on Mount Jumbo, Mount Sentinel, and land along the Clark Fork River, all then in private hands. A 1980 report by a Regional/Urban Design Assistance Team working with Missoula recommended that "no development should be allowed to mar the grassed hillsides that surround the valley in any way." The city passed bond measures to raise funds for open space acquisitions and conservation easements in 1980 and 1995, in part for scenic protection. In 1980 the focus was on acquiring land along the Clark Fork River and protecting Missoula's iconic hillsides. The 1980 $500,000 bond purchased land along the river, as well as a conservation easement on the part of Mount Sentinel facing Missoula, creating over three thousand acres of public open space. The $5 million 1995 bond gave Missoula nearly all of Mount Jumbo, Mount Sentinel, Waterworks Hill, and linear greenways in the city. It converted the Randolph homestead to public ownership. Missoula's open space bond measures were precedent-setting, inspiring other mid-sized western cities to garner public funding for wild and scenic lands.

When the city developed its 1995 open-space plan in the lead-up to the bond measure, it identified eight cornerstones surrounding the city—Mount Jumbo, Mount Sentinel, Fort Missoula, the South Hills, the North Hills, the Clark Fork and Bitterroot River corridors, recreational playing fields, and community trails. The city described these cornerstones as "giving shape to the open-space and built environment systems, making important open-space connections, serving as special local landmarks, exemplifying important natural features, offering exceptional beauty, and providing many recreational opportunities." The city now owns and manages 4200 acres of open-space conservation lands and fifty-nine miles of trails.

In 2005 and 2006, after my move back to Missoula, Five Valleys Land Trust contracted with me to manage and facilitate a citizen-driven Missoula County open-space working group. I helped the group propose a range of tools the county commissioners might use to help private landowners interested in voluntary land conservation. I traveled to all corners of the county, meeting with rural landowners. In 2006 the City of Missoula sought public input as it updated its open-space plan prior to the open-space bond vote. I participated in a public meeting of about one hundred people sponsored by the planning department. A planner showed slides describing lands at Missoula's periphery that were either protected or threatened. She showed North Hills views from multiple angles and in different seasons. One late fall image showed the North Hills from the city, with snow on Skyline Ranch's Big Pasture and none on lower Randolph Hill, now owned by the city. The speaker's point was that the snow cover happened to delineate the line where protected met unprotected land. It was a clever illustration, but misleading. Although I understood the speaker's point, I was glad that North Hills landowners were absent. This "protected" distinction at the snow line would have been an affront to the work ranchers have done to keep their land intact and working. To them, "protected" would translate to public ownership, which they oppose. This moment epitomized the gap between urban and rural values at Missoula's edge.

Although wildlife habitat and water protection drive North Hills conservation, the viewshed—a word not in North Hills ranchers' vocabularies—is a primary motivation. Websters defines a viewshed as the natural environment visible from one or more viewing points. Urban planners map viewsheds for areas of particular scenic or historic value worthy of preservation from development. Valuing the North Hills for viewshed, which does not necessarily involve owners and residents, is the opposite of valuing it for its productive potential, for "what comes off the land."

The project led to a joint city-county $10 million open-space bond measure in 2006. It focused on four main goals: water quality and wildlife habitat, working farms and ranches, open space and scenic landscapes, and trails and river access. Voters passed the most recent bond measure in 2018 with similar goals. Many taxpayers paying for open-space bond programs resist spending money to protect land on which they cannot walk, hunt, or bike. They feel that Missoulians should have access to land conserved by public money. However, in the 2006 and 2018 bond measures, voters approved funding for open-space conservation projects without public access. As people learned more about open space's intrinsic values, many of them supported funding to preserve non-recreational uses. More taxpayers now value keeping land working and protected from development, even if they are not free to walk on it. Since 2006 Missoula County has funded conservation easements on over 15,000 acres of land that have stayed in private ownership. These lands are open to the public only by invitation.

MANY POSITIVE OUTCOMES emerge from the community valuing its local open space as never before. Increasing interest in the North Hills brings resources, from open-space funding, to volunteer forces, to educational opportunities. The increased attention and use, however, is also problematic when landowners feel alienated and beleaguered. Aesthetic considerations are central to trespassers who are not content to *look* at the North Hills but wish to *be* there. This dichotomy is playing out not only for the North Hills but for rural land at the edges of many towns.

Modern ranchers' motives are not typically aesthetic. Even though they care about the view, their concerns are about remaining economically viable and keeping land in good condition. My mother wrote about the ranch's value as a community viewshed in a letter: "We have always felt there is a false collective mentality that they 'own' our place for their personal visual pleasure. 'Visual Resources' are the key words. We heard that many times in the city/county planning process." She went on to explain that she did not plan to develop the ranch, but that development was a retirement "ace in the hole." Her letter outlined how an eighty-acre section of the ranch had at one time been zoned for two dwellings per acre. She was embittered that she not only lost this liberal zoning, but a conservation strip was placed along the ranch's eastern fence line to further assure that an access road, sewer, or waterline would never cross from the Rattlesnake neighborhoods to the ranch.

A recent North Hills conservation easement further illustrates the complexities of open-space protection. Republic Services, the landfill company, bought a neighboring ranch that was accessed through the Grant Creek drainage. They placed a conservation easement on 304 acres adjoining Skyline Ranch to the west, with the intention of expanding the dump on the remaining land. A local land trust holds the easement, and the owner was compensated from 2006 open-space bond funding. As with any conservation easement, the deed restricts the amount and location of any future development. This restriction holds regardless of who owns the land in the future. This conserved property is mainly open, crossed by woody draws that provide wildlife and bird habitat and contain large ponderosa pines and intermittent springs. According to the city, "The property is visible from the large majority of all neighborhoods in Missoula. Besides the tremendous scenic

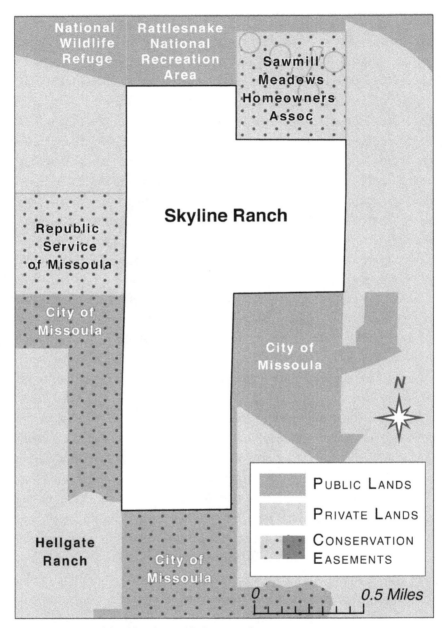

MAP 7. Conserved land bordering Skyline Ranch

viewshed value, the conservation easement will protect elk winter range, wildlife habitat and bird nesting and feeding habitat for many species, and over 120 acres of Soils of Local Importance." Note that this description does not include agriculture. The owner also committed to work with the city in granting a future public trail easement across the property.

The ranchers hanging on in the North Hills wonder: How will anyone use the conserved land, if at all? Is it still ranchland, and who will try to make a living on it? Will anyone maintain fences? Will public access bring even more pressures to our fence lines? These questions help me understand that the forces that affected my grandfather differ from the ones my mom faces. She worries about high land values (which may translate to exorbitant estate taxes at her passing). People pressure her to consider developing part of her land, while others pressure her to conserve it for elk habitat, scenic views, and recreation. Her father had none of those dilemmas.

The semantics of land conservation, protection, and preservation complicate efforts to guide landscape change. Land conservation traditionally protects natural resources from damage, which can involve directing development. Land preservation typically aims to limit human impact and forestall development. The two terms are often tossed around interchangeably.

The dichotomy of "protected" versus "unprotected" usually refers to the risk of housing development.

In the North Hills, conservation and preservation goals are compounded by protecting Missoula's view of these hills, by the desire for public trail access, and by historic preservation aims. How can we develop in ways that preserve views of the uplands? How can we compensate landowners who keep these lands open and working, encouraging wildlife habitat, water quality, and views? Volumes have been written on the ways local governments have tried to address farmland protection through regulation and incentives. For Missoula County, the conservation easement is one of the tools available to accomplish these diverse goals, and the county has used it wisely.

Of Skyline Ranch's six miles of perimeter fences, over five miles separate the ranch from conserved lands—either in public or nonprofit ownership, and/or with conservation easements. I am content that much of the

THE VIEW FROM HERE / 181

surrounding land is conserved and pleased to know that few trophy homes will sprout up as neighbors. My mom is less optimistic, feeling caught in the bullseye. She thinks the surrounding conservation pattern is limiting her options, pressuring her to provide her land for the public good. While I understand her reservations, I want what's best for these rolling hills. I want to find solutions that meld productive use of the land with preventing development and protecting views.

16

DEATH AND TAXES

It may be that the satisfaction I need depends on my going away, so that when I've gone and come back, I'll find it at home.
—Rumi

Without a doubt, people would be eager to build homes in the North Hills. While the land is valuable for the viewshed, wildlife habitat, and agriculture, some of it is flat enough to develop. Although no landowner has ever drilled a well at Skyline Ranch, and spring water is an unreliable and limited resource, well drilling may be successful. And in some western states, "dry lots" are selling well. Homes with no wells or connections to a formal water system have been approved in Arizona, with water trucked in.

North Hills access is limited. One can reach the three North Hills ranches only by passing under I-90 on Coal Mine Road. No access is possible from the Rattlesnake or Grant Creek valleys. Therefore, people must drive through the

North Side or through the industrial area west of it. The neighboring landfill is an issue; most high-end homeowners would reject homesites anywhere near it. Although the dump is distant enough to be a visual distraction only from the highest, most undevelopable areas of Skyline Ranch, one must drive by its entrance road to access all three ranches in the North Hills. Would homeowners accept that route to their homes? I believe that many would.

In 1993 Missoula County began a new subdivision process. My parents had a firm deadline for platting their ranch land before that regulation was implemented. Platting is the legal process of subdividing land into separate ownership parcels. Though my parents had no intention of developing, their attorney convinced them that the land would retain more value if they platted it into smaller parcels before the county's rules changed. He wanted a site plan to show the feasibility of developing certain parts of the ranch. He proposed creating the separate plats before the county deadline, which would make subdividing far less lengthy, complicated, and costly.

The thought of carving the ranch into building sites was loathsome. My parents wanted the land legally divided into plats but wanted to continue to own all the parcels. I did understand their motive—to keep options open and to ensure high future land values. The task of subdividing fell to the attorney. He accomplished this in time, filing the new plats only hours before the deadline. He placed a simple grid over the 880 acres of deeded land, with fourteen 40-acre splits in the Big Pasture and sixteen 20-acre lots on the lower 360 acres. The county issued thirty separate deeds in my parents' names so they could sell each parcel separately, if and when the time came. The land was now far easier to convert to large-lot residential use, was worth more, and could be taxed as building sites. The property tax rate is higher for development sites than for agricultural use. As it turned out, if my mother wanted the ranch to stay in the family rather than sell building lots, she needed the ranch to be worth less, not more. Enter the estate tax.

THE FIRST CHAPTER of Jared Diamond's 2011 book, *Collapse: How Societies Choose to Fail or Succeed*, tells the story of developers chopping up

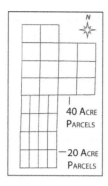

MAP 8. Skyline Ranch split into 20-acre and 40-acre parcels

Montana's beautiful Bitterroot Valley, south of Missoula. This is one case study in his treatise about societal catastrophes linked to environmental damage, climate change, population growth, and unsound political choices. It's also the story of one rancher who, like many farmers and ranchers nationwide, worried about offspring taking over the ranch. Knowing it wouldn't happen, he looked for alternatives to passing on the land. In fact, "Kids Not Taking Over the Ranch" is a common theme in most analyses of farmland loss, landscape change, and depopulation of rural places. Too often, people imply that these offspring have decided to go where the money is. They don't care about the land's productive potential but want to cash out when it's time to develop. They have abandoned their hardworking parents and turned their backs on the land.

Of course it's not so simple. I hate being lumped into a bucket with those callous "kids." Every family is different, and there are many forces at play. The family dynamics around land inheritance are difficult, whether it is a lake house that has been a family's second home for generations or a working ranch worth millions. There are complex legal and financial challenges, complicated by intense emotions, sibling rivalries, gender issues, family size, and increasing environmental challenges.

Many of those heirs, now in their fifties or sixties, are in a double bind. They can't change life choices made decades ago—decisions about partners, education, careers, and cross-country moves. Some parents encouraged them to make their own way. Offsprings' career choices were often made when the parents were still vibrant and active on the ranch. It takes deliberate decisions to go into banking or teaching rather than ranching, which is both a vocation and a lifestyle. Some, like my brother, wished to stay. However, many ranches can't support two families, or interpersonal dynamics make leaving imperative. Furthermore, ranching economics do not favor dry hillsides close to town, like Skyline Ranch. Sons and daughters often can't see a way to have an influence on what becomes of the family place.

Ideally the younger generation overlaps with the older in running the farm or ranch. Offspring often ask: "Is there a way for me to return to the ranch? Would my family dynamics make it feasible to run a business with my parents or siblings?" Offspring need a part in the decision-making and income-earning process long before their parents stop working. That's assuming the place can support more than one family. Furthermore, when land is a parent's main asset, giving up control is hard. There is so much invested—money, sweat, pride, reputations, and dreams. It's easy to understand the inherent difficulty in standing aside and helping the next generation take over. Moreover, there is no simple job description for running a farm or ranch that a parent can hand an adult son or daughter. Tasks are not defined in some corporate spreadsheet, so succession is more difficult.

The heirs dilemma deepens since a quarter of all farmers and half of agricultural landlords are sixty-five or older. Only a fraction have succession or estate plans in place. Todd Ganos, writing in *Forbes*, claims that only about one in three businesses pass to the next generation and about 10 percent to the grandchildren's generation. There is ample evidence that family wealth migrates away from those who generated it, the Rockefellers notwithstanding.

I look back and recall the opportunities and constraints that led to my leaving the ranch. While not a seamless or deliberate trajectory, some threads of my history may apply to other families. Early in my marriage, John and I leased Skyline Ranch from my parents when my dad was ill. We managed both my parents' and our own cattle herds and maintained the ranch with my parents looking on. Some families manage this intergenerational arrangement, but it is difficult. Living and working at the ranch was convenient. John was still learning the ropes, and we certainly lacked the needed capital to own a place of our own. My dad recovered, and we moved on to other rental farmsteads.

In 1975 we leased and lived on a Grass Valley ranch west of town, then we left Missoula in 1980. While we leased a ranch near Bozeman, John attended Montana State University, where he earned two degrees during the early 1980s. I milked cows and raised sheep, now with two young sons tagging along. For John, agronomy expertise and a research career served as the best surrogate for ranching. He was one of two agronomists who got their start at Skyline Ranch. Coit Suneson, Jonas's son, who left the ranch in the 1920s, was the first.

In 1986 we left ranching and Montana for more schooling. Our twenty-year marriage ended in 1992. It was twenty-five years before I moved back to Missoula with my second husband, also named John. My brother, eleven years younger than I, remained. Although he worked for a few years away from the ranch, he has spent most of his adult life working with my parents as an employee, both at the ranch and on their other properties.

Women often lack the opportunities and support needed to take over a family ranch. Although they expected that my brother would stay and work on the ranch, my parents never expected that I would do so. They did, however, assume that I'd be close enough to help out when needed. They certainly didn't foresee that I'd leave Montana. As a very young woman my mother left briefly and, after returning, she lived in Missoula for about a decade before she and my dad bought the ranch from her parents. They have been in control of the ranch, with my brother's help, ever since.

No one has made a full living from North Hills ranches since the days of my grandparents' meager living, and even they had side hustles. In thinking about succession, the older generation often worries that a son- or daughter-in-law would gain an upper hand in land management, and even ownership, through divorce. During the late 1990s and early 2000s Skyline Ranch underwent a transition period. My dad, who was seventeen years older than my mother, was elderly and ill. My parents sold the cattle herd, and the place was not producing much. They were forced to start thinking about the ranch's future use. My mother often repeats an inheritance mantra: "The first generation makes the money, the second generation builds upon it and accumulates more, and the third generation blows it." My mother remembered her parents struggling to earn the money to buy the ranch, and her own back-breaking labor building on it with my dad, and foresaw that my generation would waste it all. My aim is not to blow her wealth but to direct it toward a suitable future for the ranch.

My mother started thinking about estate planning in her late sixties. By 1999 Dad had entered his eighties and struggled through multiple surgeries and hospitalizations. At the same time that the pressure to carve a future for Skyline Ranch mounted, I was learning and teaching about farm and ranch land protection. I helped start the nonprofit Potawatomi Land Trust (now Legacy Land Conservancy), whose mission was to conserve farmland in southeastern Michigan. Looking homeward, I understood Skyline Ranch's conservation values and the mechanisms that could preserve it.

Within the family, there were shifting viewpoints. I wanted to prevent housing development in perpetuity, while my parents wanted their options kept open. By the turn of the twenty-first century, conservation organizations were calling and showing up on the doorstep with alarming regularity. My parents felt pressured by the community's desire to conserve the ranch. They resisted any notion of "locking it up" or that anyone else had a right to what they considered working land—and theirs.

In summer 2000, preparing for a vacation visit to Missoula, my mother agreed that I would set up meetings about estate planning during my stay. I accompanied Mom to visit estate planning attorneys and conservation organizations. Mom explained that goal setting was part of the problem. "We are very uncertain what we want and, what is the right thing to do now . . . We have worried for many years and attended countless meetings, constantly aware that the opportunities to do as we please with the property are eroding away with little we can do about it." This uncertainty was understandable and warranted.

We met with The Nature Conservancy, Rocky Mountain Elk Foundation, and Five Valleys Land Trust. We talked with a broker who wanted to contract with my parents to find a conservation solution. He proposed exploring options for a wildlife refuge, which was not at all what they sought. He wanted to research conservation scenarios, complete a biology study, and collaborate with various local, state, and federal agencies. His contract would prevent my parents from selling or working with any other entity for two years. They didn't hire him.

In another meeting, we met with attorneys to discuss possible estate planning approaches. In each case, my mother listened politely, divulging very little about her own assets, needs, or hopes. She became overwhelmed by the legal and financial details. Understandably, it is much easier to tackle the day's urgent "brush fires" than deal with important long-term planning. In addition, it became clear that my parents were not interested in any mechanism that "clouded the title" or gave away control or property rights. They distrusted the conservation easement tool, as many landowners do.

Protecting elk habitat was not a primary goal, as some people assumed. My mom's main concern, justifiably, was a secure future for her and her family. She made it clear there was no intention of donating rights to the land and that, indeed, it would take a large amount of money for them to consider a conservation agreement or selling out. While she anticipated great satisfaction in seeing Skyline Ranch preserved, she explained that if they needed to sell, the place would go to the highest bidder. "If that happens to be a developer, so be it."

We listed the groups interested in preserving the place as a "Visual Resource and Wildlife Habitat": City of Missoula, Missoula County, Montana State Fish and Wildlife, Five Valleys Land Trust, and Rocky Mountain Elk Foundation. She continued to list her worries: "We are undecided and that is what makes this whole situation different from when a landowner actively wants to sell . . . To do nothing closes a lot of doors . . . Pressures will continue to be put on our place to make development more expensive . . . City/county wants the place for the public to look at . . . City/county will never offer to purchase the place."

After being widowed in 2003, Mom stewed about what would become of the ranch. My brother was still working with her on her properties and was clear about wanting the ranch to stay in the family. By 2005 I had moved to Missoula, started a small consulting firm, and worked on open lands conservation in the run-up to the 2006 bond measure. I remember her coming to one of my landowner meetings at the Missoula County Extension office, where we sought input from farmers and ranchers about what they needed for making land conservation viable. She remained quiet and wary but listened.

IN 2014 my mom had become aware of the impact that estate taxes at her death could have on the ranch's future. Recent conversations with banking personnel had alarmed her about estate taxes. She warned me and my brother that we should not assume that things are going to go along the same after she's gone. She voiced the concern that the IRS could force a "fire sale" at the ranch due to the high value of the land. "There MUST be some things done, and sooner rather than later. There are decisions that must be made with and for every one of my heirs."

In 1993 my parents, guided by their attorney, wanted the ranch to be worth more and split it into twenty- and forty-acre parcels to accomplish that. Now my mom wanted it to be worth less. I imagine hundreds of ranching families going through the same discussions. Farm business succession is complicated and estate planning legalities change frequently, so planning one's estate can be a moving target. Estate taxes often prevent offspring from inheriting family land. The IRS demands that estates over a certain dollar threshold pay a tax, varying from 40–55 percent depending on the year. The threshold changes with the whims of the president and Congress. In 2014 the threshold was $5.3 million. It was as low as $600,000 in the 1990s. She worried that at her death we would need to sell the ranch quickly to pay the estate tax. Her estate will be determined not only on the ranch's value but by the sum of all her assets. Trump-era policies increased the threshold. In 2023 if you own less than about $12 million in assets, you don't have to worry about estate tax at all, but of course we didn't foresee that in 2014. Over a couple of years, she established a family partnership, whereby she donates a small percentage of the ranch to each of her heirs over a number of years. Its intent is to lower the estate tax liability. Of course a new federal administration could reduce the estate tax threshold to a low dollar figure; then she's back to square one.

It is ironic that the ranch's economic value is so high that my family risks, through estate taxes, losing property that holds so much emotional value to us, but also assets that the public holds dear—scenery, open space, and wildlife. These values are threatened as the land passes from generation to generation.

The lawyer or banker looks at land as another asset, a dollar figure in a spreadsheet of wealth. Compared with land, most assets are more fluid. Money and stocks can flow to heirs, be paid in taxes, or be given to charity—the three choices most estate planners juggle. Land is harder to pass on. With land so close to town, converting it to a fluid asset has a dramatic impact on the land and the community around it. Colliding forces of estate taxes, high property taxes, lack of farm income, and high land values create an unpredictable future. However, it is a false choice to consider only ranching and subdividing, especially on marginally productive land close to town that is not ideal for either. I imagine creative solutions around education, recreation, and local food production. Can heirs craft a solution to help keep the place in production and unpaved?

North Hills ranchers hold huge wealth in the land but don't see the world through the lens of wealthy people. Mom is attached to the ranch as a productive place, as a working, cows-on-the-land enterprise. Since that use has largely ended, it seems to her that the ranch is already gone, so she's puzzled about management going forward. Will the place be sold off one twenty- or forty-acre piece at a time? If not, who will manage it? My mom, brother, and I are united in wanting Skyline Ranch to stay in the family. But is that even possible?

I was never well-positioned to take over Skyline Ranch. Forty years after leaving Missoula, my situation is completely different—after decades careening through careers, cross-country moves, divorce, and remarriage. We now revel in a whole new generation of family, my mom's great-grandchildren. "Kids" like me from these changing ranchlands ask themselves: "What does it mean to still care? How can I influence the fate of the ranch when I do not want to be a rancher? What is my place there now? Do people like me, who leave and come back, have something special to contribute?"

Two facts remain: Skyline Ranch is still my truest home, but I don't have a place there. It's like loving an unavailable person who is vulnerable to the whims of others.

DEATH AND TAXES / 191

PART 4

RENEWAL AT THE EDGE

17

GRAVITY WINS

Autumn.
 The grace in letting dead things fall.
  —Darnell Lamont Walker

The barn was the iconic structure from the homesteading era at Skyline Ranch. My family had been watching it fall in slow motion, sagging and leaning more with each passing year. We could have started a betting pool. I would have wagered that it would fall under heavy wet snow in February. But down it went on a sunny October day in 2013. My nephew Jeremy called to tell me. He knew I was at a conference in Salt Lake City, but this was big family news. The barn was a metaphor for the ranch, with its practical utility, family legacy, and gritty handsomeness. It also symbolized the ranch's slow decline and, as it turned out, rich possibilities for renewal.

The barn that Old Man Suneson built in 1910 fell most of the way down after standing for a century. When a barn collapses, it does not fall like a set of Lincoln Logs but slumps enough to be dangerous, ending in a tangled, treacherous heap of timbers, splintered boards, and sharp, rusty spikes. Although the barn had caved in on itself, the wall separating it from an intact harness shed to the north was still standing at a slant. Old Man Suneson built the barn from two-by-twelve-foot fir planks, painted in the distant past and, in my family's time, showing only the bare red-brown and mottled gray of weathered lumber. We don't know where he bought the native fir boards, but I imagine four work horses pulling a wooden freight wagon up the dirt road from a mill in Missoula. The wagon holds a stack of rough-cut planks, six feet high and eighteen feet long.

Gravity had been gaining on the barn over the last four decades, with daylight slanting through large gaps in the roof and walls. My dad shored it up every few years, installing tight cables from wall to wall. Its further deterioration coincided with the years I was away from Missoula. It saddened me every time I arrived and saw the barn gaping open a bit more. In the early 1980s, when I was living on a ranch in Bozeman, I sent a humorous postcard to my parents. It showed a man leaning hard on the side of a barn, trying to hold up the sagging structure. "HANG IN THERE, MR FARMER!!" was printed under the photo. My parents didn't find it funny. I suppose they thought I was ridiculing my dad's efforts, but I wasn't. Granted, the postcard referenced the agricultural crisis of the 1980s—nothing to laugh at.

The barn's main open space had housed livestock and stored grain and tools. I fed my 4-H calves in the barn and brought baby lambs in for shelter during blizzards in February. Each spring, a sheep shearer bent over his clippers in the barn's doorway as we brought him one sheep after another to clip. A hayloft spanned the western third of the barn. Under the loft, walled off from the rest of the barn, a small milk parlor had a few stanchions for milking goats or cows and wooden pens for holding calves. After the barn fell, I looked over the mess many times, walking around the pile to remember its once-proud use.

The barn seemed spacious to me as a kid playing in the loft or nursing newborn calves. During haying season I struggled with hay fever, so I worked outside at the hay elevator, not up in the loft. After the collapse, the barn's open indoor space no longer existed, and it seemed a small, sad pile of wood. My dad's cables still cinched around the fallen barn like a belt around pants that have fallen to the ankles. I could see rusty metal objects amid the twisted boards, and I wanted to climb in and snoop around, but it was far too dangerous. The western side was more approachable, and I crawled in a few feet to extract a lovely rusty green bucket and a tiny cast-iron stove. My imagination fired as I found other relics that I had once used inside the barn—metal hobbles to keep milk cows from kicking, troughs for feeding grain, and chains to latch gates shut. The metal survived these many decades; anything made of rope, leather, or canvas did not.

Suneson may have built the harness shed attached to the north side of the barn at the same time as the main structure; it was there when my grandparents bought the ranch. They used it to store saddles, harnesses, and other tack. A stocky hitching post once stood outside the harness shed door but has been gone for years. After the collapse, the harness shed stayed upright and remained in fairly good shape. However, the wall that separated the harness shed from the main barn partly detached when the barn fell, so the shed was vulnerable to wet weather on its south side. When I decided to snoop inside, nobody had been in the harness shed for decades. I took shallow breaths and should have been wearing a mask. Everything was disheveled, covered in dust. I was saddened by bird droppings inches deep on the floor. I worked my way over to the horse-drawn farm wagon, built in the late 1800s. Its faded green wooden box was about four feet wide and twelve feet long. I rubbed the wood on its side with my sleeve to reveal lettering and a two-foot-wide logo. "Weber King of All" curves below a globe and the abbreviation "Est." The year has long since worn off. Mom told me that she and my dad bought it at an auction and pulled it to the ranch. Its spring seat sits askew above the wagon's box. I'm not sure they even used the wagon once.

We occasionally used the far smaller "good buggy," which was in the harness shed when my grandparents bought the ranch. Pulled by one horse, it was not a work vehicle but was used for trips to church or other special family outings in the early twentieth century. The two-wheeled cart held two adults

PHOTO 20. Barn demolition at Skyline Ranch. In this photo, the barn has been deconstructed, and the original harness shed remains standing. One of many stacks of old-growth lumber is shown in the foreground. Photo by Donna Erickson. Author's family collection.

and a couple of kids or boxes of cargo in the small box behind the spring-mounted buckboard seat. As an eleven-year-old in 1964, I sat proudly beside my mom as we rode the length of Higgins Avenue, Missoula's Main Street, in the polished buggy. The parade celebrated Montana's seventy-fifth anniversary of statehood and hundred-year anniversary as a territory. I carried a parasol and wore a pink cotton dress and bonnet modeled on late nineteenth century fashion, both sewn by my grandmother.

During the years that some semblance of a barn structure stood, my mother couldn't bear to see it torn down since it symbolized her parents' and husband's legacies. "Legacy" refers to anything handed down from the past but may also indicate something obsolete or outdated. To me, the barn signified the latter. This discrepancy raises the question of how different people honor those who came before them. My mom orients toward people's work and their possessions. To me, the barn was a sad reminder of the ranch's decline. My grandparents' work, and their love of this place, would be better preserved in my memory with the barn gone than by hanging on to it.

In October 2014, a year after the barn fell, my nephew Jeremy and I decided to work on the harness shed. Jeremy was twenty years old with a linebacker build, at six-foot-six and 320 pounds. He's the only one in the family who inherited his grandmother's red hair. We open the big wooden door, and he backs a pickup close to it. We're a good pair. He can easily handle any heavy lifting that we might encounter, but he's not small or limber enough to climb around the detritus. We want to remove things threatened by snow and rain.

Once inside, we survey the scene but can't get past the doorway. This time I wear a mask. Although it's dim inside, shafts of light angle in through gaps in the siding. Again, my heart aches at witnessing the foul state of the room. Around the wagon and buggy, harnesses and horse collars form islands in a sea of bird droppings. Dozens of spikes protrude from the walls; harnesses, ropes, gun scabbards, bridles, and cinches cover the walls in dirty dark-gray leather. Some of this stuff has been here since the 1890s. My grandfather would have used them into the 1950s. I try to recall the complicated vocabulary of harnesses— breeching, breast collar, hames, traces, belly band, surcingle, crupper, lines, blinders, martingale, spreaders—remembering names but fewer functions.

Two other large implements dominate the clutter. One is a horse-drawn stoneboat, its runners still attached. Its wooden box is a foot or so deep to hold hay, tools, or milk cans. I remember its use when I was a teenager picking rocks in the hayfield in the 1960s. The second item is an intact fanning mill, a winnowing machine used to separate chaff, dust, and weed seeds from edible grain. Farmers use this machine after the thresher has knocked the grains loose from the seed head. I imagine renewal. I want to find a new home for the mill—an agricultural museum? I snap photos with my phone.

We decide to focus on clearing the floor so we can move around. We separate debris from harnesses. Since I can more nimbly maneuver around wagon wheels, sets of buggy shafts, and broken wooden crates, I go in and pry harnesses loose from under old cowhides, scrap boards, and broken shovels. The leather is stiff, brittle, dry-rotted. Jeremy stands in the doorway to grab the harnesses from me and throws them into the bed of the pickup. We will need to sort the harnesses to decide which are in good enough shape to oil and sell. Those decisions are for another time. It's hot, dusty work. After about two hours of tugging and heaving, the truck bed is overflowing and the floor of the harness room is somewhat more clear. I pile dozens of horse collars in the buggy to get them out of the way. We intend to go back another day for harnesses hanging on the walls. We take the heaping load to the ranch's nearby granary, itself not entirely cleaned out. It's a "for now," often a defining tactic at the ranch. My mother mocks the term but keeps using it and placing things "for now."

After my session with Jeremy, I considered the barn dismantling project for a couple more years, yearning to dive in. I was in a transition toward retirement, but still busy with my consulting business and not ready to commit to a big ranch project. The blight of the collapsed structure marred the view from the house toward Lookout Hill. A niggling feeling in my bones said that the project had a deeper meaning than clearing away old boards, that it was key to my relationship with the ranch and my family. I knew it would be a huge job to take the barn the rest of the way down, sort the lumber, and pull thousands of nails, all the while keeping the pile from falling on someone's head. My brother made noises about tackling the project but didn't get around to it. He talked of using a backhoe to pull the remaining wall down, which would have ruined much of the salvageable lumber.

By February 2018 the collapsed barn had weathered almost five winters in its disheveled state, and I had retired. Should I take this on? Do I have the energy? Is this how I want to spend time in my sixties? What other projects would I forgo to do this? What help would I need? I fantasize about the neat piles of boards I could create—burn pile for the unsalvageable wood and then neat stacks of boards to keep, grouped according to dimensions: width, thickness, and length. We would sift out warped boards and those that are beautiful but not structurally sound. I am a sorter by nature.

In reality, I've been dreaming about cleaning up the ranch for the past twenty-five years. Every time I visited from afar, I walked around the ranch and imagined the sorting and cleaning I could do. The barn project, like cleaning out sheds, was a manifestation of those desires. One day I get up the nerve to ask my husband, John: "Would you be willing to help me with a project that might take the rest of my life?" Even after that ominous introduction, he agrees to help me. One motive for him is his reverence for the old-growth fir and larch, harvested over a century ago. We decide to spend one day a week at the barn, working only until tired of it. We're retired after all. As it turns out, sometimes we spend a full day and sometimes only a couple of hours.

On our first day of work, in April 2018, meadowlarks serenade us as we survey the scene and mobilize. Everywhere, the land is in spring green-up. Easter has created a mood of renewal, and I'm happy to be working outside. I'm already thankful that John bought into the project. I quickly realize that if I were doing it alone, it *would* take the rest of my life. Imagination is one thing; the reality of blistering hard work is another. Working together, classical music playing on John's cell phone, eases the physical and emotional obstacles.

We create a workstation on a flat area east of the barn. We park our thirty-year-old pickup, once my dad's ranch truck, nearby to hold tools and to haul boards home. Four sets of sawhorses create the work benches we need—one set for each of us to work at and two sets to hold boards that we pull from the barn for nail removal. Tools include what my family calls B Bars ("b" for bitch), hammers, long crow bars, and saws. We scrounge for old logs, cinder blocks, and pieces of railroad ties to stack the lumber piles on once nails are pulled. Buckets hold these nails, and we dedicate one container to interesting hardware—crusty latches, hooks, and hinges. After our first sessions, John researches the history of nails and finds that some of the ones we're pulling out—not round or square, but rectangular in cross section—were made only until the 1890s. I create a burn pile well away from the work area and garbage bins for trash. We wear old clothes and thick-soled hiking boots. I stepped on nails many times as a barefoot, careless kid; that danger is ever-present here. Mom cooks lunch for us, and I know it's her way to show support. In later weeks we bring a full meal from home and share it with her during a midday break.

It's a methodical job of harvesting boards off the structure, putting them one by one on sawhorses, and pulling the nails out. We start a pile of decent planks and another of decorative boards that have no structural integrity. I can see them reused as home decor, small shelves, or coat racks. We alternate between periods of prying boards off the barn and periods of pulling nails. My goal is to finish piling all the barn wood by the time the snow flies. It feels important to finish and I'm not sure why, except finishing brings me great satisfaction. A colleague who conducted research with me at the University of Michigan once called me the Queen of Closure. I procrastinate about starting things, but once I start, I finish. He was the opposite. It was easy for him to start but not to complete projects. We got things done!

Spikes sometimes scream as they slowly exit the wood. Other times they are barely attached, and I can pull them out with my gloved hand. Flying nails are a constant concern. When I pry one out, it is apt to go hurtling into the dirt or into my face. Over the weeks we suffer a few small injuries beyond sore muscles and fatigue. I gouge my eyebrow on a protruding nail and another day cut my lip open. I know to always pull a crowbar away from my body when pulling out a big nail. But I forgot and smashed my upper lip, just missing my teeth. The stray nails could later be a problem for livestock hooves and flat tires. We borrow a big rolling magnet, like a push lawn mower but with a cylindrical magnet that rolls across the ground. It gathers hundreds of nails into its belly.

Many boards are a delicious nutty gray-brown color. These are rough-sawn fir planks from the late nineteenth century—a 2 × 4 is actually two inches thick and four inches wide, unlike modern "dimensional" lumber, where the 2 × 4 would be 1.5 × 3.5 inches. Many are warped, although the thicker boards are straighter. We develop an eye for salvage. In a warped fifteen-foot board, we can cut a straight six- or eight-foot section. Other imperfections, like knotholes, huge nail holes and split wood, are designated "character boards." Some are unusable even for decorative purposes. The burn pile grows.

We find a large rusty piece of metal and realize it's the iron grapple fork that once lifted hay into the barn's loft. On a lunch break, Mom tells us its story. The fork, a huge pincer three feet in diameter, grabbed a mouthful of hay from the wagon, and a pulley system swung the hay up into the barn's loft. To raise the hay to the mow, Grandpa tied a rope to a horse's saddle and, as my mom led the horse away, the hook and loose hay was lifted and

PHOTO 21. Loading loose hay into the barn loft at Skyline Ranch in the 1940s. Unknown photographer. Author's family collection.

slid along a track in the barn's roof. Her sister Martha stood between Mom and the wagon and hollered for her to lead their horse Queen forward. A helper in the hayloft released a trip rope to drop the load onto the growing pile of hay.

We come across other clues to the barn's history. "Private Gym" is carved on a rafter from what was the loft. We imagine a young Coit Suneson, probably in the 1910s, sweating up there as he did pull-ups on the big beam. I don't remember seeing the carved words when I played and worked in the loft.

Certain tasks take more strength than I have, especially in dealing with the "big uglies"—sistered joists attached together lengthwise for greater load-bearing. Builders nailed, and sometimes screwed, them many times along their lengths. We must pry or saw off metal joist hangers at the ends. We lack a power source, so a battery-powered reciprocating saw is our only mechanization for slicing these joints apart. A division of labor emerges in our partnership, and the "big uglies" are all John's.

One May day we hear a groaning rumble behind us as we stand at our sawhorse stations pulling nails. The fifteen-foot wall separating the barn from the harness shed has been hanging at a sagging angle above a tangle of barn wood. We turn and realize the wall is falling. We are fifteen feet away, so we don't get caught in the falling debris. We have been taking one board at a time from the barn skeleton, always aware that removing one board could cause the wall's collapse. One of those detached boards, or a slight breeze, has triggered a final collapse. Startled, our first question is "where's Blue?" My mom's Australian shepherd loves watching us work from a shady nook underneath leaning boards. We encourage her to lie in other shady places, but she loves this precarious cubby hole. She was chasing deer when the wall fell, so she's fine. We're happy that the barn's skeleton is now far safer for all three of us.

We photograph the scene as we're cleaning up and putting away tools each session. I envision a flip-book showing the barn disappearing from April to October. The photos show the ground greening up and then dying back as summer blooms then wanes. They capture cloudscapes, from filmy cirrus to billowing cumulus, above our project: we try to pick dry, warm days to head to the ranch. By late spring, our wood stacks are almost hidden by the yellow blooms of mustard and other weeds. Other than the knee-high green grasses and weeds, the scene is gray—gray boards, metal roofing, tools, and tarps. We can see the barn shrinking and the piles of lumber growing. We whet our appetites by setting arbitrary markers: "It will be fun when we can get to that wall and salvage those red tongue-and-groove boards."

We are about half done on June 14. Occasionally John goes to the ranch another time or two in a given week and works alone. He has developed the closure bug too. The barn's main outside walls and its roof are nearly gone. We worked from the uphill, eastern side through May and then moved to the lower western side and made good progress there. My notes from that June day: "Right now we have stacks of boards with nails to pull, boards with nails removed leaned against the harness shed wall, stacks of old tires, a couple more rusty stoves. We can now almost walk from west to east side through

204 / RENEWAL AT THE EDGE

what was the barn's floor. The interior wall of the milk house is impeding us. Good boards on it, so that will be fun to dismantle, as well as south wall of harness shed—beautiful straight boards."

By fall, we enjoy a view from the house unblemished by the splintered barn. The change is dramatic. It shows that positive transformation can happen, that empty space can symbolize growth. We finish by mid-October and cover four large piles of wood with tarps. We haul a couple of pickup loads to our home in town and devise a good system for storage. We didn't have a firm plan for the wood and still don't. I've sold boards at my antique mall booth, and customers love them for little projects. Most buyers get only one or two boards. We reuse special boards as tabletops, coatracks, and shelves, my imagination fueled by beauty and possibility.

Later that winter, record-setting snow blanketed Missoula. The snow drifted three or four feet high over our careful wood piles. The high winds twisted and shredded our tarps. The snow was so deep it was difficult to even get to the piles to re-cover them, but I managed to keep them protected. Those old boards have survived for over a century. They'll keep weathering, waiting for the perfect new application.

The barn demolition was a labor of love. It expressed my affection for the ranch and honored the North Hills ranchers' legacy of "just-getting-by." It felt gratifying to work at the ranch on a focused project after decades away. Late in the fall my brother, Ken, and his son Jeremy built a hay shed on the exact footprint of the barn. They attached it to the south side of the harness shed as the barn had originally been. I was pleased that our project led to rebirth. A new generation of family will stack hay bales in the exact part of the barn where my grandfather brought his loose alfalfa to stockpile over long Montana winters.

OF RUIN AND RENEWAL

We are souls
Of ruin and renewal
Sorting through the rubble
Of our painful past.

We are souls
Of ruin and renewal
Waiting for the dust
To settle at last

We are souls
Of ruin and renewal
Searching for eyes that see us
And walk through the debris

We are souls
Of ruin and renewal,
We rebuild, we revive,
We repurpose our own story."

—Liz Newman, *Of Ruin and Renewal: Poems for Rebuilding.* 2019

18

BLUEBIRD DAYS

The bluebird carries the sky on his back.
—Henry David Thoreau

As I write, it has been exactly eighty years since my grandparents bought Skyline Ranch. I've recorded this landscape's stories from my perspective, illustrated by my own experiences and memories and relying on family lore passed down incompletely and perhaps inaccurately. This book presents snapshots in time, not necessarily linear or complete. Looking back at North Hills history is like looking through an antique glass window, where objects blur and lines distort. Looking forward, the window becomes nearly opaque, but I can make out important shapes and hope they come into better focus during my lifetime and those of my sons and grandchildren.

I don't know who will own and love these hills, how the ranches will be managed, and what decisions will change the land. In 2023 I own 6 percent of Skyline Ranch through our family partnership, not enough to give me much say in what happens. Though I'd like to predict the changes awaiting the North Hills ranches, it would be foolhardy. Besides, there is no end state; the landscape will always evolve. New generations of people will take control and make changes.

What I *can* do is hope. Or call it visioning, dreaming, strategizing. As William Randolph dreamed of inventing new subsistence schemes for mining and farming, I want to create something new in the North Hills. Buckminster Fuller said: "You never change things by fighting the existing reality. To change something, build a new model that makes the existing model obsolete." If North Hills families and the Missoula community want to use and protect the North Hills, the current owners and the community must build a new model, grounded in the desires of the two remaining North Hills families, limitations of these dry hills at the edge of town, and the City of Missoula's twenty-first century demands. I'm seeking directions and priorities, not solutions or mandates, and I realize that my family members may not share my perspectives. These visions came into focus during hikes I took during six months of 2020, the first Covid 19 pandemic year.

Because of the pandemic, I felt vulnerable, uncertain, worried. These feelings mirrored my apprehensions about the future of Skyline Ranch and the North Hills. Due to the stay-at-home orders in Montana from March through May, people started using the city's trail systems in record numbers. On trails, we could leave our houses in a relatively safe space. There was so much increased trail use, the city installed signs: "Keep right except to pass," "Uphill hikers have right-of-way," "Physical distancing," "Don't stop on the trail," and "Don't linger at the trailhead." After a few weeks in lock-down, I started hiking the hills surrounding Missoula myself, for mental health and for the healing quality of movement and nature. I hiked with a cloth mask over my mouth and nose.

May 26, 2020: Mount Sentinel Fire Road. As I leave my car and set off on Mount Sentinel's steep uphill trail, the clock tower on the University of Montana's Main Hall starts ringing. I count each chime, already knowing it is 7:00

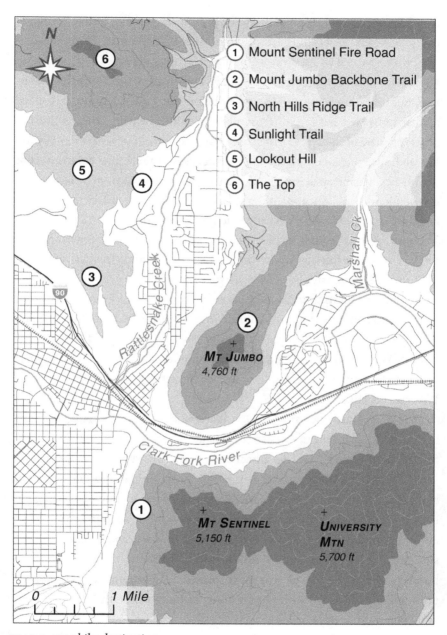

MAP 9. 2020 hike destinations

a.m. Mount Sentinel is Missoula's most prominent symbol, visible on nearly every postcard. Open hillsides provide Missoula's popular hiking destination, where we feel we are away from Missoula, but still part of it. It's a still day with wispy clouds in the west. The sun has not yet emerged over the mountain, but it brightens most of the valley below me. I don't let myself stop for a break until I reach a specific fence post. Breathing heavily, I turn to face the soothing view of the North Hills. I see dappled sun about where the Skyline Ranch house tucks behind the hill. Farther west, thin smoke columns from the plywood plant catch my eye. The only other visible movements are semis on the freeway, and once again I'm struck by the clear boundary the highway creates between Missoula's North Side neighborhood and the North Hills. The buff-colored landfill disturbance stands out from the greener artificial terraces near the freeway where the waste disposal company has reclaimed land after filling massive trenches with garbage.

I climb off the trail to let runners pass and then wait a few minutes for the air to clear of possible virus-infused droplets. After an hour, I start seeing more people on the trail. Higher up, my eyes scan north toward the soft contours of Waterworks Hill and the southern mound of Randolph Hill beyond it. I spot the shiny round flying saucer of the city's covered water tank on Waterworks Hill.

The exaggerated two-track on the Waterworks Hill ridge continues onto higher Randolph Hill then becomes a single track pointing farther north, toward our property line. As a backdrop, snow still sparkles in the Rattlesnake Mountains. Pivoting back to the trail, I see Lolo Peak to the south still blanketed in snow. The meadowlarks' song is soothing and joyful, sending me back to childhood on the ranch. Another bird—or is it a ground squirrel?—emits a periodic chirp that seems to originate in low grasses. Sentinel's hillside is a shower of blooming yellow arrowleaf balsamroot. Purple lupine is budding out at the top of gray-green plants. Likewise, yarrow is popping up—dull-green foliage with pin cushions of buds where the white flowers will open in a few days.

An hour into the hike and it's far easier. Now fully in the sun, I'm on a two-track fire break road that crosses the mountainside, so the route is nearly level. My mind wanders to the future and the hopes I have for the North Hills. My ardent desire is that houses do not dot those hillsides and that the view from town remains intact, even for, or especially for, those thousands who do not venture off the valley floor. I know that landowners must be compensated for the lost development opportunity. Looking at the still North Hills scene from a distance, I can feel the resistance building inside me. I want the view to stay the same, the form to remain unchanged but the function to improve. Protecting the view is the easiest goal to propose and probably the hardest to accomplish.

Stopping again to take in the scene, I see the North Hills forming a calm painted stage set behind the City of Missoula. I don't think many Missoula residents understand what has gone on in these hills. I can see myself as a girl, riding horseback on a mild June day to gather cattle for branding. The hikers I'm passing don't know about the rancher mowing hay in one of the wetter meadows tucked between hills. Few Missoula residents know that my nephew gets up in the middle of a frigid February night to check for new calves. I wonder if many hikers worry about houses someday sprouting in the North Hills, as they've appeared on Missoula's South Hills for many decades.

At 9:00 a.m. I am back at the car. The hike provided a much-needed fresh perspective on the North Hills from across the valley. It's easier to visualize my wishes for the North Hills' future by being physically separate from them. It is like leaving Missoula for twenty-five years to pursue education and a career, then coming back with a new mindset. The hike stimulated new thinking about the use and protection of the serene hills north of town.

June 1, 2020: Mount Jumbo Backbone Trail. A week later I've decided to climb to the top of Mount Jumbo for a closer look at the North Hills. I can choose to climb Jumbo from its front or back. The southwestern slope facing town is a steep climb to the white concrete "L" on the open, grassy face of the mountain, followed by a strenuous trudge to the top. I've chosen the back route, which starts near a saddle between the mountain's north and south summits and climbs the Backbone Trail through ponderosa pine and Douglas fir. It's a beautiful hike, although some steep pitches challenge my sixty-seven-year-old knees.

BLUEBIRD DAYS / 211

For me, Mount Jumbo embodies Missoula's relationship with its native fauna. From December 1 to May 1 each year, the mountain is closed for hiking to protect the Mount Jumbo elk herd grazing on its winter range. When snow is too deep for elk to forage at the higher elevations, they move lower on the slopes of the mountain, just as the North Hills elk herd moves onto ranchland from the Rattlesnake Wilderness. From the valley, we don't need binoculars to see elk grazing above Rattlesnake neighborhoods. Mountain lions prowl the high country close to town and, when food is scarce, they hunt in the lower Rattlesnake Valley at the base of Jumbo. People occasionally spot wolves in these hills around Missoula. Even grizzly bears are far closer to western Montana's valleys than they were in the past. These megafauna species will likely create even more contentious conservation battles.

It is a sweet irony that wildflowers high on the hillsides are so lush and plentiful in this pandemic year. We need that joy. Not only are the flowers abundant but species that are usually spread out on the spring and summer calendar are blooming simultaneously this spring. As I hike the saddle and up onto Jumbo's ridge, I see glorious fields of prairie smoke, Indian paintbrush, bluebells, and shooting stars. I see my first larkspur of the year. Larkspur was the nickname 4-H friends gave me as a kid.

I wonder what climate change will mean for these native species, here on Jumbo and in the North Hills. Adaptation is basic to biology and a key concept for responding to climate change. Over many generations, species become better suited to changing habitats or they die out. Can the native species of the North Hills persist with the increasing pressures generated so close to the city? I hope these hills—and especially their native flora and fauna—will adapt in some fashion to the coming heat. Can humans adapt to these changes as well?

In recent years Mount Jumbo and Mount Sentinel have been periodically closed to hiking during the height of the fire season to protect people from wildfire. People can be in peril if caught on these dry slopes when a wind-driven fire speeds uphill. When I consider the North Hills' future, increased fire danger is a given. Massive conflagrations could obliterate buildings. Fire would spread up the dry, grassy slopes and into the forest, unstoppable except by rain or a cold front. I hope the railroad ties that my grandfather set as fence posts remain unburned! Eradicating flammable weeds is one defense against looming fire danger. Unfortunately, near the trailhead today, I saw dried invasive knapweed plants from last year, with green shoots at their bases. While North Hills ranchers have made progress on weeds, there is much more work to do. I imagine bringing sheep back to help control weeds naturally on many of the slopes surrounding Missoula.

Nearing Jumbo's summit, I enjoy another spectacular view: west toward the North Hills, a bit closer than the view from Mount Sentinel, with the Rattlesnake Valley in the foreground below me. Mount Jumbo mirrors many North Hills environmental issues, but without the ranching history. Far more than fire, or even agricultural use, housing development is a great danger to natural systems, a threat that has been eliminated for Mount Jumbo by conservation easements and public ownership. I'm thankful for the conservation of this elephant-shaped hill. I'm also grateful to be breathing clean air up here. We used to smell the pulp mill west of town, so I'm aware that environmental improvement is possible.

The North Hills, however, are still threatened. While housing developments will increase to the east of the North Hills, in the Rattlesnake Valley, and to the west in the Grant Creek drainage, a wedge of North Hills land could remain open, anchored by Waterworks Hill and the Moon-Randolph Homestead. I can see it from the top of Jumbo—a wide swath of land kept open as a living, breathing ecological gradient connecting the city to the wilderness. The corridor, already partly protected, would be a wedge four miles wide at the freeway and connecting, to the north, with US Forest Service land and the Rattlesnake Recreation Area. In this future scenario, only the most limited, deliberate, and sensitive developments would be created. As I imagine this gradient from the city to the wilderness, I breathe easier, feeling relief, security, and calm.

JUNE 3, 2020: North Hills Ridge Trail. Two days after my Jumbo hike, I decide to take a close-up look at what I've been eyeing from across the valley. The trailhead sign says the Moon-Randolph Homestead is a two-mile walk and the summit is one mile away. The trail up Waterworks Hill is far wider than when I learned geology up here with Bruce Baty over ten years ago. Large stones, a foot or more in diameter, line each side of the trail to discourage people from wandering off. They seem to be working. A train whistle blares from the tracks below me, and other whirring sounds announce a city at work. Some noise carries from the freeway, but another constant background hum is hard to pinpoint.

I see the spot where the peace sign once stood. It has been nearly twenty years since it was dismantled. Its message lives on. The Jeannette Rankin Peace Center bought a small piece of land on the side of Waterworks Hill directly above downtown Missoula. It built a far smaller peace sign on a whitewashed rock to pay tribute to the iconic original, which endures as a Missoula symbol on T-shirts, bumper stickers, license plates, and postcards.

High on Randolph Hill, I get one of the best 360-degree views of the Missoula region. After spinning around to take it in, I look down and am distressed to see invasive leafy spurge starting to bud. Yarrow and Missoula phlox are now in full bloom. I pass an older gentleman with two walking sticks and a severe limp. He's veering off the trail to let another hiker pass with the prescribed six feet of social distancing for Covid 19 safety. I approach the upended rusty car chassis, eight feet tall, that creates a fitting gateway to the original Randolph ranch, now City of Missoula open space. The sculptural metal frame is another symbol of the North Hills, planted there many decades ago by the Randolphs. Their motives were surely functional—repurposing old materials for fencing. But they must have had an artistic impulse as well. The whimsical gateway reminds me of Cadillac Ranch, the 1974 Texas art installation of upended Cadillacs in the desert. The Randolphs' work pre-dated it by decades. That thought gets me humming Bruce Springsteen's "Cadillac Ranch" for much of the remaining hike.

Of my spring hikes, this one provides the best view yet of all three ranches. Now I can see the North Hills' lay of the land and witness the heavy trail use. Passive recreation, which does not require special facilities or equipment, will remain an important use for the North Hills landscape, and I wish we could extend hiking access northward from this heavily used trail on Randolph Hill. I worry about unintended consequences. Can recreational access coexist with agricultural goals and ecosystem protection? The challenge, of course, is managing access to private land in a way that minimizes damage and overuse.

Being up on Randolph Hill reminds me that, beyond recreation, there is so much to learn and interpret here—not just the geology I learned with Baty but also the natural and cultural history that shapes this landscape. The Randolph Homestead has changed the least over the past twenty years, continuing the historical interpretation and education that has been its purpose since Bill Randolph's passing in the 1990s. Through living-history demonstrations, the legacy of innovation, reuse, and "getting by" is visible at the Homestead and informs people about dwindling resources and the need to conserve during the Great Depression era and beyond.

Adults and kids could follow the Native American trails that crossed the North Hills before white settlements, learning about ancient migration routes. Building on the Homestead in new ways, people could learn about the mining era on these ranches and see demonstrations of weed control, ecological restoration, controlled burning, water development, and alternative energy. Children need tours of the landfill as much as they do an apple orchard. Learning about forest management could be a focus in the Big Pasture. Venturing farther north, naturalists could guide walks to study North Hills geology and flora.

My brainstorm at the top of Randolph Hill is about the inherent tension between progress/development and conservation. Earlier chapters suggested that trespassing, hunting, and dog walking are problematic, with thoughts of keeping people *out*. I dream of the North Hills landscape as intact, enriched by inviting a larger number of Missoulians *in*, not only to use the land but to love and steward it. Education is key to that goal. When I witness the Homestead's successful programs—whether birding walks or orchard management—I can imagine spreading these themes further into the North Hills, with other types of learning, topics, and experiences. The North Hills are rife with possibilities for even more connections to Missoula through education.

There is another antecedent for education in the North Hills, a place I can see as I look north from Waterworks Hill. The Rattlesnake Wilderness was dedicated partly around an educational agenda. Former congressman Pat Williams from Montana, with others, worked to promote the wilderness as a center for environmental education, given its proximity to Missoula. The 1979 Rattlesnake Education, Recreation and Wilderness Area Act promoted wilderness designation and outlined a list of reasons to protect the Rattlesnake. The first was to "promote, support, encourage, and increase public awareness and understanding of the significance of wildlands as a national resource." Williams wanted the Rattlesnake region to be a national model for using the wilderness as a classroom.

July 1, 2020: Sunlight Trail. A month elapses before I get out hiking again. Today I opt for a popular trailhead on the west side of the upper Rattlesnake Valley. At 7:00 a.m. mine is the only car in the small lot. Later on, hikers will struggle to find parking. From the start of the trail, I see the Lone Pine far uphill to the west. The trail shoots straight toward it as if it were a terminus. From here, the Lone Pine's babies look almost as big as the mama. As I get closer, it's clear that the young trees are only half as big. They are all on the eastern, city, open-space side of the fence, maybe because grazing on the Skyline Ranch side thwarts seedlings. Perhaps the westerly winds blow the Lone Pine's seeds eastward. It feels odd to walk toward the ranch from here, but it is the route that many of our neighbors take to hike near the North Hills, and I want to experience it. This is my first time at Sunlight Basin, a city-owned open space.

When I was young, this was the Papoose Pony Ranch, which raised and boarded horses and took people on trail rides. In my mom's youth it was the Clover Leaf Dairy. Now the public open space is conserved for wildlife habitat and for Missoulians to hike on. Both my mother and I rode across this land many times as girls and young women, when neighborly relationships were the norm. Times change. Our history with neighbors in the eastern Rattlesnake Valley has not been positive in more recent decades, whether over stray bulls, loose dogs, or trespassing. On the way up the trail, I pass the dried and empty flower stems of arrowleaf balsamroot, twisting three feet or more into the air. Two young women pass me, heading toward our fence line. I give them a wide berth as their three German shepherds run around me unleashed. I try to ignore the licking, nosing, flailing dogs as I recall the trials we endured fifty years ago when marauding dogs sprinted up this same hill to massacre my sheep.

When I reach the Lone Pine, I stay on the public side of the fence, although I long to crawl through the barbed wire and embrace the tree's scaly bark. I don't want other hikers to cross the fence behind me or chew me out for doing so, not knowing that it is my family's land. As I face the Lone Pine looking west, to my right and behind me is the 229-acre Sunlight Basin property, through which the trail loops before returning to the trailhead. To my left is a 150-foot-wide conservation corridor along our fence line—the strip my mom complains about because it prevents Skyline Ranch from ever gaining access to utilities from the ranch's eastern side.

From the fence in front of the Lone Pine, I look down into the hayfield where I picked rocks as a kid, now weedy and overgrown. My family's cows are grazing contentedly. Nearer to where I stand, the impromptu skating rink where my grandkids skated a few years ago is now full of blooming invasive leafy spurge. At the fence separating our Hundred and Sixty from this public land, a stone about eighteen inches in diameter is wired to the bottom strand of fence wire to pull it down. Barbed wire wraps around the rock in both directions like a present's ribbon. At first I think it was hung there by my grandfather, but then I notice that the fence posts are not wooden. My brother and my son Rye rebuilt this fence line in the 1990s using metal posts. They've used one of our grandfather's fencing "hacks."

Not far from the hanging stone, a wooden birdhouse is attached to a fence post and has a small metal strap with the words "In memory of Elizabeth Johnson." This is box number N3, put here by Mountain Bluebird Trails, a conservation organization dedicated to bluebird recovery. A small note on the box's side claims forty-five western bluebirds have fledged from the box. Johnson began putting up the boxes along this fence line in 1998. Western Montana has both mountain and western bluebirds; the small bright blue thrushes fly north from Mexico in late February and early March. Bluebird habitat diminished over many decades due to the removal of nesting trees, particularly snags with cavities made by woodpeckers. Agricultural pesticides also contributed to their demise. I'm so pleased that they are making a comeback.

I'm heartened by the land conservation at Sunlight Basin but saddened that none of the original Clover Leaf Dairy buildings remain to give any hint of the varied human histories on this property. It makes me hope that farming and ranching families continue to live in the North Hills, even as the landscape is further conserved. Several large new homes cluster near the open-space corridor. Other than the caretakers at the Moon-Randolph Homestead, the folks in these homes are my mom's closest neighbors. They don't feel like neighbors, since they drive to their houses from the Rattlesnake Valley, miles away from North Hills access on Coal Mine Road. Lifestyles of North Hills ranchers vary dramatically from those of professionals in these suburban homes. Although I feel that neighborliness is important, melding white- and blue-collar sensibilities in this context is challenging, at best.

However, these neighbors may share common concerns with North Hills ranchers. Foremost, they may hate to see further housing development in the North Hills. They probably want to close that door behind themselves. No one can ignore the rampant housing development since the pandemic. Missoula is in a frenzy to build affordable and "workforce" housing through promoting infill and by approving large apartment blocks, some at the edges of town. One subsidized development is just breaking ground. It will shelter those households earning 30–60 percent of Missoula's median income. It is tucked right up to the freeway at the edge of the North Side. The North Hills will surely be those peoples' backyard, creating even more need for neighborly cooperation and respect.

Rattlesnake neighbors are likely concerned about preventing wildfire and weeds. Everyone likely shares an appreciation for the North Hills elk herd and other wildlife. These homeowners may also be concerned about trespassing, roaming dogs, and unauthorized hunting. Given these shared interests, how can neighborliness exist in new ways?

I imagine inviting these neighbors to the Randolph Homestead, where we could talk about North Hills wildlife issues, fire prevention, and other concerns. Neighborliness can coincide with recreation and education. Neighbors in the Rattlesnake Valley can be informed about acceptable practices on the different types of land in the North Hills—private land (with and without public access), city open space, and federal recreation land. Some of this neighborly communication and collaboration can be done in tandem with recreational activities like sledding parties, holiday events, and harvest days. Amiable cooperation is a nicety, but it's also a necessity if a new North Hills model is to be possible.

August 5, 2020: Lookout Hill. Another month has passed, and I am walking to the top of Lookout Hill at Skyline Ranch. We're in the dog days of summer, the driest, hottest stretch. The Old Farmer's Almanac defines the dog days as the period beginning July 3 and ending August 11, a span that coincides with the rising of the dog star, Sirius, at sunrise. It's been scorching hot lately—most days over 90 degrees Fahrenheit. At midday, the ranch feels empty, asleep. I'm on a two-track through an old hayfield with Canada thistles growing five feet high on both sides. They are contorted and brown because the weed spraying contractor my mom hired doused them a couple of weeks ago from a tank on his four-wheeler. In addition, the road I'm walking on has nearly a monoculture of knapweed on both sides.

Thousands of grasshoppers jumping through dried grass sound like pages turning in a dusty old book. Hundreds of them bounce off my knees as I walk along. Fire danger is high because fuel is dense and crisp. My mood is melancholy because the land seems dormant and vulnerable. It is quiet, except for the beep-beeping of garbage trucks, as they back into the landfill over a mile away, and the occasional meadowlark aria.

I'm climbing uphill to get the closest North Hills perspective yet in my summer hikes. From Lookout Hill, I have a perfect view of the Randolph Homestead, largely unchanged since I was young. Closer, on Skyline Ranch, I'm proud to see the new hay barn, but the slew of sheds, most with fringes of detritus and old vehicles, is a visual affront. A large field near the horse arena harbors hay equipment, an uninhabitable trailer house, and dozens of junker cars. The time and effort I've put toward cleaning the place is a drop in the bucket; it needs a lot more work to become functional. Today I focus on an imaginary view.

BLUEBIRD DAYS / 219

I want to see the North Hills *used* again. The ranches have lain fallow for too long. The Randolph Homestead has found its use. When I think of all the possible futures for these lands, conjuring productivity feels the most certain and concrete. The loose sketches in my head include cattle and sheep grazing, fruit and vegetable crops feeding a hungry town, and people actively working the land. I imagine women farming, just as my grandmother, mother, and I did for so many decades. Could we renew connections to the North Side and other neighborhoods north of the Clark Fork River, where homesteaders once sold produce, hired workers, and hosted work days? I yearn for hospitable and supportive connections to these gritty working-class neighborhoods based on food production.

The North Hills can come full circle, contributing to the local, sustainable, farm-to-table food movement. These hills may be more important than ever for growing food for Missoula. I dream of a healthy inventory of "what comes off the land" in future decades. This is not the best farmland in the Missoula region, but its virtue is proximity to where people live. My productivity vision depends on costly and time-consuming infrastructure development. Fences must be maintained and better water sources explored; those two tasks are only a start.

Hiking back down toward the ranch house, I walk along the draw that ends at the barnyard. Shady and dense, it's impossible to walk down into it, but I see limbs moving and a rustle of activity. Mom's cattle are at the bottom, thrashing around, maybe to seek shade. A big ponderosa pine, twice the size of the Lone Pine, stands sentinel at the southern end of the draw near the spring where the ranch house's potable water emerges. Water is the linchpin of life in the North Hills, scarce but critical for both housing and agriculture. While the existing springs are useful, if somewhat unreliable, more water would be a game-changer in the North Hills. A 2019 hydrological study at Skyline Ranch already shows where well drilling is likely to be successful, at least for livestock water and limited irrigation. Renewable technologies can be used to catch rain and to pump and deliver water using alternative power from the sun and wind.

Important principles practiced by the homesteaders will be renewed— crop diversity, agricultural innovation, and the value of outdoor work. Health is at the heart of it—health of the land, the people farming it, and local eaters. Farmers could innovate with the types of food that can be grown in these hills, using an appropriate balance of cultivated and grazing land. Jonas Suneson, William Randolph Sr., and Gustav Carlson grew raspberries, rhubarb, asparagus, potatoes, beef, and eggs to sell in Missoula. What other crops might be viable on this less-than-prime farm ground? Further, the link between productivity and education has outstanding potential. Young new farmers can learn the farming craft, local neighbors can become educated on home gardening, and children can experience harvesting vegetables. The Peas Farm in the Rattlesnake Valley, run by the University of Montana and the nonprofit Garden City Harvest, is a great local model.

Farmers should not break ground that's never been plowed. I'd hope that crops can be grown on land that produced crops before, land now supporting weeds. Most of the North Hills landscape is prime grazing land. My mom has a few head of cattle now, and Hellgate Ranch still supports about forty head. The need for local sources of beef, processed by small facilities, is more apparent than ever in this pandemic year. The meat packing industry is being hamstrung by Covid 19, where viral outbreaks had closed 216 plants in thirty-three states by June of 2020. The U.S. is now relying on foreign sources of beef more than ever.

A carrying capacity analysis could show how many cow-calf pairs could graze these hills. Their movements could be monitored by a rotational grazing system that directs livestock to specific areas. Managers of the North Hills, including my family members, could introduce more livestock—sheep, goats, pigs—and include "value added" practices whereby raw meat products are processed to yield a higher market value. Heritage cattle breeds such as Kerry and Canadienne could be a focus, with an aim to conserve historic breeds and genetic diversity. Kids will laugh at the Dutch Belted cows, which look like giant Oreos. Similar approaches could be used with weed-eating sheep and other livestock. This vision requires active managers and reliable teams of workers. Teenagers' 4-H projects might help implement improvements and monitor production and ecosystem health. Haphazard management will fail this close to town. People see and appreciate active management—whether fence maintenance, weed eradication, or livestock husbandry. They respond by checking their own behavior to avoid trespassing and other inappropriate activities. Careful management will be critical for supporting food production, education, and other positive changes in the North Hills.

OCTOBER 27, 2020: *Hike to The Top at Skyline Ranch.* Many weeks have passed since my summer hikes, and it is an unsettling time. The pandemic is in a second surge, and the election season has been brutal. Hunting season opened last weekend, and I'm wearing an orange plastic safety vest as I hike the south-to-north length of the ranch. It's midmorning on a "bluebird day"—deep blue sky and cloudless. My brother was in the Big Pasture much earlier this morning, seeking to fill his elk tag. Like our grandfather, he feeds his family partly by stocking the freezer with game each fall. It's surprising that he's seen no sign of the elk herd. The first killing frost came late, just a few days ago, accompanied by nearly a foot of snow in the Missoula valley. Most snow has melted in town, but it is still two inches deep up here. I stay warm by walking fast, following the knobs and swales of the Hundred and Sixty and Big Pasture in the same pattern I once traced with Blue. Tawny dried grasses reach up nearly to my shoulders. I stay on the two-track road I know so well. It has been sixteen years since my trip up here with Rye, he on his bike and me in the old ranch pickup. I am so grateful to know this land that grounds me to my family and my own story. It feels that time nearly stands still when I'm up here.

My sensory connections to the ranch include the sight of gentle landforms. My memories include the aroma of newly mown alfalfa, the sound of bleating lambs, the taste of fresh-picked raspberries, and the feel of sticky hound's-tongue on my blue jeans. But other senses besides those basic five are processed in our brains. Chronoception refers to perceiving the passage of time. Decades ago, it was the feeling of the day slipping by while I bucked bales in the hayfield. Now I sense the decades falling away behind me as I ponder what the ranch has meant to me for almost seventy years.

On my way to The Top, I'm thinking about our upcoming elections and the devastation of Covid 19. It makes me think back to *Living the Good Life:*

How to Live Sanely and Simply in a Troubled World, which I first read at the ranch in the early 1970s. For Helen and Scott Nearing, their 1932 move from New York City to a farm in Vermont's Green Mountains was a "personal search for a simple, satisfying life on the land . . ." They were escaping a society gripped by depression, fascism, and the threat of another world war. We live in a world troubled in ways the Nearings could not have foreseen, adding climate change, nuclear war threats, and viral pandemics to the list of worries. My vision for the North Hills is partly informed by the Nearings, hoping for rich human experiences and healthy ecosystems.

The irony is not lost on me that thousands of people have flocked to Montana seeking the good life during and after the Covid pandemic. Montana towns, like other western destinations, have been discovered. An outcome of the pandemic has been an influx of people escaping cities, working remotely, and seeking retirement homes near natural beauty. In 2021 my husband, a baseball fan, heard an advertisement for the state of Montana in a Pittsburgh Pirates telecast. Add the lure of the popular TV series *Yellowstone*, and we see more and more people coveting a Montana lifestyle. A University of Montana study found that the Yellowstone series has generated over two million visitors to Montana, accounting for $730 million in revenue. People are visiting, but then wanting to stay; in 2021 the ratio was 7:1 of people moving into and out of Montana.

MY SUMMER HIKES yielded five big visions, merely raw sketches of a new model. The future of North Hills ranches might include elements of scenery, stewardship, education and recreation, neighborliness, and productivity. Some priorities are compatible, overlapping to form a quilt of sustainable use. Others are at odds, at least on the same patch of ground. Elk habitat is consistent with protecting the view and with livestock grazing, but not with growing row crops. Recreation can create neighborly connections but is more difficult to provide near sensitive native plant communities. Rich possibilities exist for combining education with agricultural production. One pairing is striking: cows and bluebirds coexist well. Many bluebird trail boxes are on grazing land since cattle keep grass short, helping birds find insects.

Underlying my rough model, I wish to embrace and build on Missoulians' interest in the North Hills. Supplementing the unique Moon-Randolph Homestead partnership, and the investments Missoulians have already made in that ranch, we could build a coalition for the larger North Hills region. I imagine an agricultural district for ecosystem conservation, sustainable agriculture, and community health. For the North Hills to be a stronger community asset, innovative partnerships and investments could assure that landowners' needs are respected and the public benefits. Furthermore, my goals are generalizable to the broader western landscape. Many other rural western towns with ranching, mining, and logging histories face the same dilemmas. For the North Hills, as at many western edges, the land's future is at a tipping point.

Skyline Ranch may be the hub for new activities that bring people into the North Hills. In my mind's eye I see a new red barn near the ranch house, combining the latest green technology with Scandinavian vernacular design that honors the original homesteaders. At Hellgate Ranch, the core settled area with the original brick house and Archie's home is likely to remain in the Carlson family. Grazing will be the main use on several hundred acres, but the realist in me knows that the landfill's owners will likely buy acreage north of the ranch houses for dump expansion.

Perhaps the district could have a formal home, such as a heritage center to coordinate programming for production, education, recreation, and environmental protection. Where the Moon-Randolph Homestead looks fondly back at a history of self-sufficiency and innovation, the demonstrations at the other two North Hills ranches can look forward, adding more layers to the same themes—contemporary green technology, adaptation to global climate change, sustainable agriculture, ecological restoration, and green building. Let's focus on the edge: it's where interesting things happen.

My vision may be unrealistic. As my heart pumps hard on the last steep stretch to The Top, I'm also heavy-hearted about what is likely to happen in the North Hills, and specifically at Skyline Ranch. What will my family decide? But I still dream of community-minded outcomes. I imagine what my grandparents would want to happen, and I'm sure they would endorse keeping cattle, horses, crops, and ranchers thriving in the North Hills. They would want Missoula's northern skyline to remain unblemished. I believe that many people are eager to join together and address the unique opportunities and challenges at these edges, to keep the skyline open.

At the ranch's highest point, I sit to take in the view at the same spot where I rested Blue decades ago. Clean, frosty air fills my lungs. Viewed from town, the Big Pasture is still white with snow, while it has melted in the valley, creating that line that the Missoula County planner once referenced as a conservation boundary. I look across at Mount Sentinel, where a large black twenty-five-acre patch burned on August 21 after kids played with a cigarette lighter at the base of the mountain. As usual, the fire traveled uphill, so it did not endanger homes below it, but emergency responders hit it hard from the ground and with an air attack of helicopters and tanker planes. Thankfully, firefighters stopped the flames at the fire break road I had hiked on in the spring.

I'm spooked by hearing a rifle shot in the distance and don't feel safe at the edge of the forest. I start back down the hill. After another hour of walking, I circle to the Lone Pine, where I take a moment to gaze into the Rattlesnake Valley, lingering under the tree's sheltering branches for a few moments. My ashes will someday be spread here. As we head into the winter following an especially difficult year worldwide, the ranch can once again go to sleep and await spring and the bluebirds' return.

My totem animal would be the bluebird. Some Native American tribes honor the bluebird as an important omen. Their legends show reverence for the bluebird as a symbol of hope, renewal, and prosperity. We associate the color blue with bright sky, azure oceans, and the concepts of loyalty, peace, and serenity. Through time, the bluebird has stirred those traits, plus a childish innocence, in people's imaginations. And they're not even blue! Bluebirds' feathers are not pigmented blue. The color is produced by the structure of the feathers, which scatter blue light and absorb other wavelengths. The blue is a trick of light. The bluebirds' most beautiful and recognizable feature is an illusion, as is much that we hold dear.

BLUEBIRD DAYS / 225

As I reflect on my years in Missoula's North Hills, I keep coming back to the bluebird. Twisting the "bluebird of happiness" idiom, Woody Allen said: "Early in life I was visited by the bluebird of anxiety." When it comes to the future of the North Hills, I share those ambiguous feelings. However, in framing my vision for North Hills renewal, I choose the bluebird of happiness . . . and beauty . . . and community. The bird is my emblem for a promising future in the North Hills.

"HOPE" IS THE THING WITH FEATHERS

Hope is the thing with feathers
That perches in the soul
And sings the tune without the words
And never stops at all.

And sweetest—in the Gale—is heard—
And sore must be the storm—
That could abash the little Bird
That kept so many warm—

I've heard it in the chillest land—
And on the strangest Sea—
Yet—never—in Extremity,
It asked a crumb—of me.

—Emily Dickinson, *The Complete Works of Emily Dickinson*, 1983

EPILOGUE

After all, hope is a form of planning. If our hopes weren't already real within us, we couldn't even hope them.
—Gloria Steinem

Change continues to subtly shape the North Hills. Dramatic alterations have not occurred in the 2020s, but rather a slow transformation that pulls the landscape further from its ranching heritage. Biological threats continue. The Lone Pine appears sick, evidenced by the foliage's gradual color change—turning a dull yellow green and then reddish brown as the Mountain Pine Beetle burrows under its scaly bark. Similarly, many ponderosa and lodgepole pines in the Big Pasture are dead or dying of the same infestation. I struggle not to interpret the Lone Pine's declining health as a symbol for the North Hills future. Optimistically, small pines continue to sprout up on the hillside below the Lone Pine, and adolescent trees appear to thrive. Renewal is possible.

Meanwhile, life goes on in the North Hills for a handful of people. At Skyline Ranch, the land's future remains in limbo as my mother nears ninety. Large-lot landowners are building homes and roads across from the ranch's northwestern and southeastern fence lines, on the only land bordering the ranch that is not conserved or in public hands. Threats of drought and wildfire persist. A trespasser started a fire in the Big Pasture in March 2024, burning eight acres near Bear Draw. Luckily, the fire only affected one big ponderosa pine. I'll be watching to see if more native grasses emerge from the burnt grassy hillside.

Few cattle graze the North Hills' grassy hillsides. The closing of the Missoula Stockyard in 2024 is further evidence of the cattle industry's decline in western Montana. Mom sold her cattle in 2023 but continues to rent grazing rights to a rancher who pastures cattle during the summer months. It brings me pleasure to know that the rancher raises only natural, grass-finished beef, sold locally. This circles back to the work of earlier generations. In addition, the income generated from renting pasture assures that the land is assessed at the agricultural, not development, property tax rate.

At Hellgate Ranch, an important relic of the North Hills' coal mining era ended when a deconstruction company tore down the big coal bin at the Carlsons' place. It is gratifying to know that those massive timbers, over a century old, were reused and honored in some creative way. The Carlson brothers died in the early 2000s. Walter's sister and other heirs own and manage the land. Archie's cattle were sold following his death. The landfill inches northward toward Hellgate Ranch on Republic Services land. We have been told that the landfill will move its dump access, in about 2030, to Grant Creek Road, where a freeway interchange gives better access. If this occurs, the company will close its current dump entrance on Coal Mine Road, halting the continual stream of garbage trucks and reverting the North Hills to a quieter corner of Missoula. In summer 2024, Hellgate Ranch is for sale, throwing its future into more uncertainty.

West of Hellgate Ranch, the City of Missoula and Five Valleys Land Trust locked in another piece of the North Hills conservation puzzle in 2019. The 125-acre Bluebird Preserve serves the rapidly expanding population in the

Grant Creek drainage and on Missoula's far west side. Open space bond funding made the project a reality. Trails on the scenic North Hills preserve will eventually connect to new trails on the 304 acres of conserved land owned by Republic Services just north of Hellgate Ranch.

The Moon-Randolph Homestead continues its stable, ongoing purpose of educating Missoula about the legacy of homesteaders and early ranchers. The sheep have returned to the homestead, grazing the hillsides and helping to control weeds. More people than ever hike the public trails at the homestead, aided somewhat by the reconstruction of the Waterworks trailhead in 2022. The homestead welcomed almost 2600 visitors in 2023, a third to half of them children. People interact with the land through open Saturdays, concerts, weddings, summer camps, and field trips. The two women caretakers host events with topics ranging from photography to pruning to art. This couple has worked and lived at the homestead for seven years, the longest tenure among the seven caretakers/couples who have served in that role. The peace sign that formerly overlooked the city from Waterworks Hill was stored for twenty years and reassembled in 2021. It now stands as a twenty-four-foot-tall permanent art installation in an alley behind the Jeannette Rankin Peace Center in downtown Missoula, just a block from the Clark Fork River.

Three years after my pandemic hikes in 2020, Missoula's housing shortage has put even more pressure on undeveloped lands, as Missoulians see a shortage of houses for sale, a growing population, exorbitant rents, and record home sale prices. Home values increased 57 percent from January 2020 to January 2022, according to the Missoula Organization of Realtors, and the housing inventory declined 58 percent. The median house price was $550,000 in 2023; one-third were cash sales. According to the *Montana Free Press*, "Missoula is one of many metropolitan areas where the real estate market looks increasingly like San Francisco's, especially after the pandemic and the rise of remote work led some people to leave cities in search of more space and cheaper home prices." Short-term rentals have also added to the price hike.

What sets Missoula apart, though, is the availability of land close to town. Pressure mounts to increase the pace of development on nearby open lands and on city infill. Both the City and County of Missoula are overhauling zoning codes to propel development. Residents of the Villagio Apartments are the newest neighbors near the North Hills. The two-hundred-unit affordable housing project, tucked snugly next to the freeway off Coal Mine Road, began housing low-income Missoulians in 2023. Hundreds of new neighbors will live a stone's throw from the three North Hills ranches.

Meanwhile, as Missoula grows and its population expands, interest and investment in local food is skyrocketing. Simultaneously with promoting housing development, the city prioritizes local food production. The city and county created a Food Policy Board in 2020 to support, among other things, vibrant local food systems and small farming enterprises. The steady greening of Missoula is due, in large part, to an ecosystem of local food-related non-profits like Garden City Harvest, Community Food and Agriculture Coalition, and Missoula Farmers Market. The city partners with these groups to promote direct sales, community-supported agriculture (CSAs), and community gardens. Perhaps the North Hills will be one location where these priorities take root in the twenty-first century.

Meanwhile I stay rooted in Missoula and continue to admire the view north of my home in town. I hike the North Hills, take my grandkids to The Top, and savor the peaceful flow of the landscape. I will do whatever I can to promote good decisions at this important edge.

www.ingramcontent.com/pod-product-compliance
Lightning Source LLC
Chambersburg PA
CBHW030908110225
21631CB00014B/42